CONTENTS

ABOUT THIS BOOK

This *Step by Step Guide* has been produced by the editors of Insight Guides, whose books have set the standard for visual travel guides since 1970. With top-quality photography and authoritative recommendations, this guidebook brings you the very best of Barcelona in a series of 19 tailor-made tours.

WALKS AND TOURS

The tours in this book provide something to suit all budgets, tastes and trip lengths. As well as covering Barcelona's many classic attractions, the routes track lesser-known sights and up- and coming areas; there are also excursions for those who want to extend their visit outside the city.

The tours embrace a range of interests, so whether you are a fan of art or architecture, a gourmet, or have kids to entertain, you will find an option to suit.

We recommend that you read the whole of a tour before setting out. This should help you to familiarise yourself with the route and enable you to plan where to stop for refreshments – options for this are shown in the

'Food and Drink' boxes, recognisable by the knife and fork sign, on most pages.

For our pick of the walks by theme, consult Recommended Tours For… *(see pp.6–7)*.

OVERVIEW

The tours are set in context by this introductory section, which gives an overview of the city, plus background information on food and drink, shopping, entertainment, Modernisme architecture and the Catalan language. A succinct history timeline highlights the key events that have shaped Barcelona over the centuries.

DIRECTORY

Also supporting the tours is the Directory chapter, comprising a user-friendly A–Z of practical information, our pick of where to stay, and select restaurant listings; these eateries complement the more low-key cafés and restaurants that feature within the tours themselves and are intended to offer a wider choice for evening dining. A selection of nightlife listings rounds off your trip.

Above from top: signs advertising the Museu Marítim; sunbathing on the waterfront boardwalk; Catalan Renaissance-style arches of the Plaça del Rei; port-side dining; stylish light in Antoni Gaudí's La Pedrera.

The Authors

Roger Williams came to know and love Barcelona during frequent visits to the city from his home on the Costa Brava. He is continually delighted by its contradictions and describes it as a city that is at once one of the most bourgeois in the world and also one of the most avant-garde.

This new edition of the book has been thoroughly updated by Jackie Staddon and Hilary Weston, who enjoy returning regularly to Barcelona to reacquaint themselves with old favourites and seek out new surprises, which this ever-evolving city constantly delivers, because Barcelona never stays still.

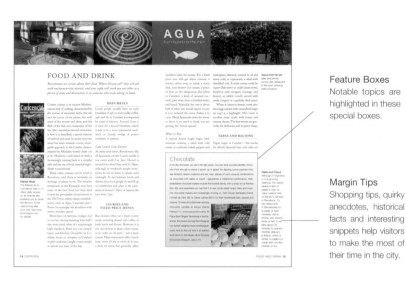

Feature Boxes
Notable topics are highlighted in these special boxes.

Margin Tips
Shopping tips, quirky anecdotes, historical facts and interesting snippets help visitors to make the most of their time in the city.

Key Facts Box
This box gives details of the distance covered on the tour, plus an estimate of how long it should take. It also states where the route starts and finishes, and gives key travel information such as which days are best to do the route or handy transport tips.

Route Map
Detailed cartography shows the itinerary clearly plotted with numbered dots. For more detailed mapping, see the pull-out map slotted inside the back cover.

Food and Drink
Recommendations of where to stop for refreshment are given in these boxes. The numbers prior to each café/restaurant name link to references in the main text. Places recommended en route are also plotted on the maps. Note that in Spain, addresses marked 's/n' have no house number.

The € signs given in each entry reflect the approximate cost of a three-course, à la carte dinner for one, with a bottle of house wine. These should be seen as a guide only. Price ranges, which are also quoted on the inside back flap for easy reference, are as follows:

€€€€ €60 and above
€€€ €40–60
€€ €25–40
€ €25 and below

Footers
The footers on left-hand pages give the itinerary name, plus, where relevant, a map reference; those on the right-hand pages cite the main attraction on the double page.

ARCHITECTURE

From pure Catalan Gothic around the Royal Palace (walk 2) to the Modernista showcases of the Eixample (walk 10), including Barcelona's greatest work-in-progress, the Sagrada Família (walk 11).

RECOMMENDED TOURS FOR...

ART BUFFS

Artistic highlights include the Museu Picasso (walk 5) and Monjuïc's Fundacío Miró (walk 12); the latter tour also visits the Palau Nacional, home to the world's best collection of Romanesque art. For the lowdown on Salvador Dalí, there is a trip to Figueres (tour 19).

FAMILIES WITH KIDS

There is lots to appeal, including the wax museum (walk 1), the boating lake in Parc de la Ciutadella (walk 8), the beach (walk 9), Barça football club (tour 13) and CosmoCaixa science museum and Tibidabo funfair (walk 16).

FLORA AND FAUNA

For a spot of greenery, to look for parakeets, or to check out the zoo, visit the Parc de la Ciutadella (walk 8). Horticultural lovers should head for the various gardens on hilly Montjuïc (walk 12).

FOOD AND DRINK

Sample the excellent tapas on and around the Passeig de Gràcia (walk 10) or slip up to Gràcia (walk 15) for a drink in one of the area's many authentic local bars. Trips further afield include a tour of Catalonia's wine region (tour 18).

MUSIC LOVERS

El Liceu opera house (walk 1) and the gorgeous Modernista Palau de la Música Catalana (walk 4) should be top of your list. Also recommended is the wonderful music museum, the Museu de la Música (walk 8), north of Parc de la Ciutadella.

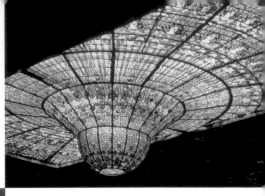

NIGHT OWLS

You will find places that open late across the city, but good starting points for night-time action include El Born (walk 5) and La Rambla (walk 1), which is busy day and night. Or chill out by the waterfront at Port Olímpic (walk 9).

RAINY DAYS

Sit it out in the larger institutions such as the Museu d'Art Contemporani de Barcelona and the Centre de Cultura Contemporània de Barcelona (walk 6) or the Museu Nacional d'Art de Catalunya, in the Palau Nacional (walk 12). Alternatively, combine shopping at the waterfront Maremàgnum mall with a visit to the aquarium (walk 7).

ROMANCE

Buy flowers on La Rambla (walk 1), take a boat trip on a Golondrina (walk 7) or watch the pretty, illuminated waters of the Font Màgica de Montjuïc (walk 12).

SPORTY TYPES

Visit the buildings erected for the 1992 Olympics and check out the Museu Olímpic i de l'Esport at Montjuïc (walk 12) or pay homage to Barça football club at Camp Nou (walk 13).

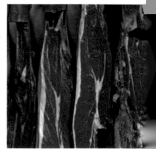

OVERVIEW

An overview of Barcelona's geography, customs and culture, plus illuminating background information on food and drink, shopping, entertainment, architecture, language and history.

CITY INTRODUCTION

A vibrant, dynamic city, always on the move but passionately guarding its heritage, Barcelona offers everything from Gothic treasures and traditional dances to trendy bars, innovative architecture and gorgeous food.

When anyone asks what are the best things to see in Barcelona, the answer should always be: just walk the streets. Few cities in the world are so agreeable for simply wandering, thanks to Barcelona's rich architectural heritage, from giant Roman stones and sunless medieval lanes to the brilliant architecture of Gaudí and the Modernistas, and the shimmering, sharp-edged 21st-century blocks that are placed with such panache alongside the historical gems.

DEVELOPMENT

Lying on the Mediterranean coast in northeast Spain, some 260km (160 miles) from France and a distance of 625km (390 miles) from Madrid, Spain's second-largest city was founded by the Romans. The *oppidum* of Barcino was entrenched behind walls encircling the area around what is now the cathedral and the government buildings of Plaça de Sant Jaume. During medieval times – Catalonia's Golden Age – the Counts of Barcelona pushed the walls south beyond the famous La Rambla avenue, to encompass El Raval and create what is now the whole of the old town, or Ciutat Vella. Beyond this lay the hillside Jewish burial grounds of Montjuïc.

The 19th Century

Towards the end of the 19th century a vast new extension (Eixample) was laid out in an impeccable grid system inland, while an industrial area spread north alongside the shore. The Ciutat Vella, the Eixample (where Antoni Gaudí's Sagrada Família and many of the Modernista showcase buildings are located) and the former industrial area

Above: port cable car; Modernista sign; Tibidabo funfair.

Late Habits
Everything starts late in Barcelona: lunch is not usually until 2pm and dinner not until at least 9pm or 10pm, which is when most concerts start. Live-music venues and clubs do not get going until 2am. Pace yourself with a few tapas.

Right: Mercat de Santa Caterina.

that has been transformed into a beach front (Barceloneta and the port) are the three key areas that most visitors come to explore.

NAVIGATING THE CITY

Centred on the Plaça de Catalunya that separates the old part of town from the new, Barcelona is an easy city to navigate. The grid system of the Eixample is simple to follow, and though the lanes of the Ciutat Vella are more maze like, that is half the fun. A good way to get to know your way around is to take a ride on the tourist bus, which passes all the main sights, where you can hop on and off. Taking a trip around the port in a Golondrina pleasure boat is another way to get a sense of the city, while cable cars and funiculars whisk you up to its high spots for bird's-eye views.

If you head up to the castle at the top of Montjuïc, you can see the city stretching far to the south, beyond the commercial port, down to the Llobregat River. In the other direction, heading north, if you walk the whole length of the beach you will eventually arrive at the new Forum and the River Bésos, marking the city's northern edge. The Serra Collserola, with Tibidabo's Sagrat Cor church pricking the skyline, stops the city from expanding far inland.

Public Transport

The transport system, including a highly efficient metro network, is straightforward to navigate. Metro, rail and bus services are all paid for using the same tickets, which are compara-tively inexpensive, especially if you buy them in blocks of 10. For more information on this, consult the Directory chapter (see p.109).

THE BARRIOS

In spite of the city's size, the communities and villages that make up Barcelona give it an intimate feel. These *barrios* (districts) have strong identities and flavours, celebrating their own festivals and making their own entertainment, for example. Usually

The phrase *Vaig de bòlit*, meaning 'I'm speeding', is used by busy Barcelonans, who live with what George Orwell called 'a passionate energy'. They like to be viewed as *espavilat*: dynamic, assertive and productive.

Below: stylish local walking her dog.

centred on a square or two, where the outdoor seating that is common in Barcelona allows people to stop for a chat, these *barrios* maintain their individuality. And with a mild climate and temperatures rarely falling below 10°C (50°F) in winter, and rising to 25°C (77°F) in summer, it is not surprising that people spend much of their time outdoors. Wherever you stay in the city, you are soon likely to find a favourite street or square with a bar or café where regulars gather for a morning *cortado* (coffee) or lunch-time ice cream. And you will soon find yourself slipping into the rhythm of late starts (shops open around 10am), quiet afternoons and buzzing early evenings, when everyone seems to be out and about for a stroll in the city's streets.

STRONG HERITAGE

Like the city's numerous long-established cafés and bars, many shops seem rooted in the past. It is hard to think of a major city that maintains so many specialist shops: a *pollería* selling nothing but chicken; a *cuchillería* selling knives, a *colmado* that stocks only dried goods. The influx of immigrants has only added to this mix. The city's commercial individuality is borne out, too, with the modern boutiques and one-off designer outlets of El Raval and El Born, where small premises are often just a workshop with a window.

CREATIVE SPIRIT

Diseny (design) is the most pervasive talent in a city that has produced some explosive creativity, in both the plastic and performing arts. The national characteristic is said to be a mix of *seny* (wisdom) and *rauxa* – a kind of wildness that produces creativity. It results in a mix of deep conservatism and mercurial flair, which might explain the Sagrada Família, an extraordinary avant-garde work by a deeply religious traditionalist. It perhaps also explains the city's history, a mix of highs and lows, of times of great prosperity and times of gruelling hardship, times of enlightened thinking and times of incendiary passion.

URBAN PLANNING

The city's urban planning is a match for its architectural bravura. Barcelona is a city whose planners take bold steps, in spite of frequent opposition. They are unafraid to pull down great chunks of old properties and replace them with cutting-edge modern buildings, or simply leave breathing spaces.

Growth Spurts

The city has grown in bursts: the Golden Age of the 13th and 14th centuries produced the Gothic mansions of the Ciutat Vella. Architectural development was low-key until the 19th-century industrial boom funded the Modernista extravaganza of the Eixample. In the mid-20th century, however, the fascist dictator General Franco put a stop to just about everything. In the second half of the 20th century, while other European cities were ripping out their architectural heritage and throwing up skyscrapers, Barcelona languished, unloved by the holders of the national purse strings.

It was not until 1986 and the prospect of the Olympic Games that the city reawakened, attracting architects of the highest calibre in a second *Renaixença* (Renaissance).

A Dynamic City

After years of stagnation and recession, the city is on the move again. The focus is on the two main arteries running east–west to the sea, Avinguda Diagonal and Avinguda Paral.lel, creating a cohesive connection to the port with its cruise-ship terminal, and the Forum's trade fair, exhibition and conference venues. The former industrial area, Poble Nou, has either been cleared or had its factories converted to make way for a high-tech explosion. Supporting all this are new transport links, both over and underground. Debate rages as to whether this will destroy the authentic spirit of Barcelona or happily co-exist with its industrial heritage.

Festivals and Partying

The Barcelonans like to party, and barely a month goes by without some excuse for a celebration. Each district's *festa major* (main festival) involves large family meals, dishes and pastries created specially for the occasion, plus crates of cava and lots of music. The city's principal festival is the week-long La Mercè in September, with spectacular parades of 'giants', 'dragons' and 'devils' with music and dance and fireworks. In addition to this the festive calendar is marked with celebrations at Carnival, just before Lent, and the eve of the Feast of St John, on 23 June. Two peculiarly Catalan contributions to the party scene are the traditional *sardana* dance (see p.38) and *castells,* human 'towers' that reach five people high. More tranquil is the celebration of St George, patron of Catalonia, when red roses and books are given as gifts (see p.45).

FOOD AND DRINK

Barcelonans are serious about their food. 'Where did you eat?' they will ask with uncharacteristic interest, and your reply will mark you out either as a person of taste and distinction or as someone who needs taking in hand.

Market Meals
The Mercat de la Concepció *(see p.71)* offers daily recipes on its internet site, enabling you to recall the flavours of Barcelona long after your visit. See www.laconcepcio.com for details.

Catalan cuisine is an ancient Mediterranean style of cooking, characterised by the aromas of mountain herbs, the oils and the juices of the plains, the wild meat of the woods and skies, and the flesh of the fish and crustaceans of the sea. *Mar i muntanya* (sea and mountain) is how it is described, a special mixture of seafood and meat. In recent years the trend has been towards a more avant-garde approach to the Catalan classics, inspired by Michelin-starred chefs *(see p.16)*. However, a new breed of chefs is increasingly turning back to a simpler style and the use of local, seasonal ingredients is paramount.

Many other cuisines can be tried in Barcelona, and there is certainly no shortage of places to eat. The smarter restaurants in the Eixample may have some of the best food, but they tend to lack the personality of restaurants in the Old Town, where classic establishments such as Agut, Caracoles and 7 Portes increasingly rub shoulders with newer, trendier places.

Most bars (or *tabernas*, *bodegas* and *cervecerías*, the last meaning 'beer hall') also serve food, often of a surprisingly high standard. Here you can sample tapas, sandwiches (*bocadillos* in Castilian, *bocats* or *entrepans* in Catalan) or *plats combinats* (single-course meals) at almost any time of the day.

MAIN MEALS

Local people usually have an early breakfast of *café con leche* (milky coffee, *cafè amb llet* in Catalan) accompanied by toast or biscuits. Around 11am it is time for a second breakfast, which tends to be a more substantial sandwich or chunky wedge of potato omelette, or pastries.

Late Lunch, Late Dinner

At other meal times, Barcelonans, like all Spaniards, eat late. Lunch usually is not eaten until 2 or 3pm. Dinner is served from about 9pm until 11.30pm, although at weekends people sometimes do not sit down to dinner until midnight. To last between lunch and dinner, do as local people do and fill up on sandwiches and cakes in the patisseries at around 5.30pm, or tapas in the bars from 7pm.

COURSES AND FIXED-PRICE MENUS

Barcelonans often eat a three-course meal, including dessert and coffee, at both lunch and dinner. However, it is not uncommon to share a first course, or to order *un sólo plato* – just a main course. Many restaurants offer a lunch time *menú del día* or *menú de la casa*, a daily set menu that generally offers

AGUA
bar·tapes·restaurant

excellent value for money. For a fixed price you will get three courses: a starter, often soup or salad, a main dish, and dessert (ice cream, a piece of fruit or the ubiquitous *flan* (*flam* in Catalan), a kind of caramel custard), plus wine, beer or bottled water, and bread. Typically, the cost is about half of what you would expect to pay if you ordered the same dishes à la carte. Many Spaniards order the *menú*, so there is no need to think you are getting the 'tourist special'.

What to Eat
A typical dinner might begin with *amanida catalana*, a salad with cold meats; or *escalivada*, baked peppers and aubergines, skinned, covered in oil and eaten cold; or *esqueixada*, a salad with shredded cod. A main course could be *suquet* (fish stew) or *estofat* (meat stew), *botifarra amb mongetes* (sausage and beans), or rabbit *(conill)*, served with snails *(cargols)* or a garlicky alioli sauce.

When it comes to dessert, *crema catalana* (egg custard with caramelised sugar on top) is a highlight. *Mel i mato* is another treat, made with honey and creamy cheese. The best sweets are generally the delicacies sold in pastry shops.

TAPAS AND RACIONES

Tapas (*tapes* in Catalan) – the snacks for which Spanish bars and cafés are

Above from far left: beer and *jamón*; *xurros*; fish restaurant in the port; enticing fresh produce.

Chocolate

If you like chocolate, you are in the right place. You can drink *xocolata desfeta,* chocolate thick enough to stand a spoon up in (great for dipping *xurros* pastries into), see fantastic festive creations and eat main dishes of such unusual combinations as chocolate with rabbit or squid – apparently a traditional combination. Well-established chocolate makers include the Escribà family, with a shop on La Rambla (No. 83), and elsewhere you can find it in raw, brick-sized lumps. New and inventive chocolate makers are increasingly moving in. Visit Cacao Sampaka (Carrer Consell de Cent 292 or Carrer Laforja 96) to try their handmade bars, sauces and creams. Or taste chocolate beer and buy chocolate candles at Xocoa (Carrer Petrixol 11; www.xocoa-bcn.com). At Plaça Sant Gregori Taumaturg in the Eixample, the award-winning Oriol Balaguer has further delights (www.oriolbalaguer.com). And to find out how it all started, stroll down to the Museu de la Xocolata (Chocolate Museum, *see p.47*).

Paella and Fideuá
Although it originates in rice-growing Valencia, the classic seafood dish of paella is high on many visitors' lists of dishes to sample in Barcelona. Try the restaurants in Barceloneta for a paella of fresh mussels, clams, shrimp and several kinds of fish. It will take about 20 minutes to prepare. Another delicacy is *fideuá*, which is similar to paella but made with noodles instead of rice.

Michelin Stars
In 2012 the number of Michelin-starred restaurants in Barcelona and its immediate environs stood at 18, with two restaurants having two stars: Abac, headed by sensational young chef Jodi Cruz, and Lasarte. The other 16 have one star each. The majority of these restaurants are in luxury hotels in the Eixample district. Since the closure of world-renowned El Bulli in 2011, there remain just two three-starred restaurants in Catalonia: Sant Pau and El Celler de Can Roca. The influence of El Bulli chef Ferran Adrià has been immense; his approach to cooking has seen a fleet of new chefs bringing an avant-garde technique to their dishes. There has, however, been a trend to return to traditional cooking using high quality and seasonal produce, especially from chefs such as Carme Ruscalleda of the three-starred Sant Pau. This is highlighted in her new restaurant, one-star Moments in Eixample, where her son Raül Balam is head chef.

world-famous – come in dozens of delicious varieties, from appetisers such as olives and salted almonds, to vegetable salads, fried squid, garlicky shrimps, lobster mayonnaise, meatballs, spiced potatoes, wedges of omelette, sliced sausage and cheese. The list is endless, and can be surprisingly creative, especially at the now extremely popular Basque tapas joints, where they are called *pintxos*.

A dish larger than a *tapa* is called a *porción*. A complete serving, meant to be shared, is a *ración*, and half of this, a *media ración*. Tapas are usually available throughout the day, and provide a great way to sample new dishes.

They can also be filling, especially when eaten with a chunk of Catalonia's best invention, *pa amb tomàquet*, bread rubbed with garlic, olive oil and tomato. This bread is particularly good, too, with ham *(pernil)*, spicy sausage *(xoriço)*, cheese *(formatge)* or anchovies *(anxoves)*.

Other dishes to point to on the bar might be *truites* (*tortillas* in Spanish: omelettes made with potato and onion, and sometimes also with spinach); small fried fish; octopus; snails; or *patates braves*, potatoes in a hot tomato sauce.

DRINKS

Wine, Cava and Beers

Wine is a constant at the Catalan table. In addition to a wide assortment of fine wines from across Spain, including Rioja, Navarra and Ribera del Duero, Barcelona has some extremely good regional wines. Those from Penedès, the grape-growing region

just outside Barcelona where cava, Spain's sparkling wine, is produced, are excellent *(see pp. 94–5)*. Cava itself goes wonderfully with seafood and most tapas. Among Penedès reds, try Torres Gran Coronas, Raimat and Jean León.

Wines from the Priorat area, around an hour to the south of Barcelona (near Tarragona), are superb, robust, expensive reds that rival the best in Spain. Do not be surprised to be offered red wine *(vi negre)* chilled in hot weather. There are also several delicious, dry rosés *(vi rosat)* from the region.

Spanish beers, which are available in bottles and on draft, are generally light and refreshing.

Other Alcoholic Drinks

Sangría, made of wine and fruit fortified with brandy, is drunk more by visitors than local people. More popular among the locals is sherry *(jerez)*, of which you will find every kind here. Pale, dry *fino* is drunk not only as an aperitif but also with soup and fish courses. Rich dark *oloroso* goes particularly well after dinner. Brandy is another option as a *digestif*: Spanish brandy varies from excellent to rough: you usually get what you pay for. Other spirits are made under licence in Spain, and are usually cheap.

Hot Drinks

Coffee is typically served black *(solo)*, with a spot of milk *(cortado/tallat)*, or half and half with hot milk *(con leche/ amb llet)*. *Orxata*, made with ground tiger nuts and milk, is also popular, and is served both hot and cold.

Typical Menu Items in Catalan

Entrants/Primer Plat (Starter/First Course)

amanida green salad

arros negre black rice, squid and its ink

canelons a la barcelonina cannelloni stuffed with meat

cigrons chick-peas, often stewed with chard *(bledes)*, spinach, tiny clams or cod

croquetes cassolanes homemade croquettes (with chicken, ham or salt cod)

empedrat white bean salad with tomatoes, onions, salt cod and olives

escudella thick soup with noodles, made from stock produced when boiling meat

espinacs a la catalana steamed spinach, lightly fried with raisins and pine nuts

faves a la catalana broad beans, stewed like lentils

gaspatxo Andalucian cold tomato soup

llenties lentils, usually with spicy sausage and black pudding

sopa de peix fish soup

verdures vegetable of the day, often overcooked with potatoes

Segon Plat (Main Course)

calamars a la romana/farcits squid fried in batter or stuffed

fetge liver

fricandó braised veal with wild mushrooms

mandonguilles meatballs

peix (lluç, tonyina, gambes, sèpia…) a la planxa fish (hake, tuna, prawns, cuttlefish) cooked on a griddle; meat (notably rabbit) is also cooked this way

pollastre rostit chicken roasted in a rich sauce

pollastre/carn arrebossada chicken/meat (usually beef) fried in breadcrumbs

salsitxes amb tomàquet thin sausages in tomato sauce

xai a la brasa lamb cooked on open wood or charcoal fire

Postre (Dessert)

flan crème caramel

fruite (poma, platan, pressec, sindria) fresh fruit (apple, banana, peach, watermelon)

gelat ice cream

macedonia fruit salad

mel i mató creamy curd cheese with honey

postre de music nuts and dried fruits, often served with moscatel (dessert wine)

pastis tart/cake

Above from far left: paella; chocolates; lunch on the beach; tempting tapas.

Below: cava and tapas for the masses.

SHOPPING

Barcelona is a great place to shop, from its innovative, design-conscious showcases around the Passeig de Gràcia and Diagonal to the timeless independent shops in the Barri Gòtic and cutting-edge boutiques in El Born.

In keeping with its reputation as a centre for style and design, Barcelona has an impressive range of fashion boutiques, antiques shops, state-of-the-art home interior stores and art galleries. Shopping is extremely pleasant here, as the city has not been totally overtaken by homogenous chain stores and still has many quirky and enticing family-owned shops. The best items to buy include trendy clothing, shoes and other leather products, antiques, books (Barcelona is the publishing capital of Spain), high-tech design and home furnishings.

SHOPPING AREAS

The Passeig de Gràcia, Rambla de Catalunya and interconnecting streets are good for chain stores, high-end fashions and boutiques. The same goes for the Barri Gòtic, which also has many artisanal shops, galleries and trendy souvenir sellers, plus hip clothes stores as you move towards El Born. The Avinguda Diagonal, from the top of Rambla de Catalunya to the roundabout that forms Plaça Francesc Macià, and the streets behind, are good for fashion at the top end of the market, while Gràcia is a relaxed place to shop, with cutting-edge young designer fashion and jewellery. The new Arenas de Barcelona

complex, in the old bullring building in Plaça d'Espanya, has a good range of popular brands and speciality shops.

DEPARTMENT STORES

The largest department store in Barcelona is El Corte Inglés, with a branch in Plaça de Catalunya, another in nearby Portal de l'Angel specialising in leisure, music, books and sports, and others in Avinguda Diagonal. All branches are open Monday to Saturday, from 10am till 10pm. The branches on the Plaça de Catalunya and Diagonal (No. 617) have excellent supermarkets.

FASHION

Designer Clothes
Antonio Miró (no relation to the artist) is perhaps the most famous Catalan designer of men's- and women's-wear, with clothes characterised by low-key design and clean lines. His shop can be found at Carrer del Consell de Cent 349. Other designer names to look for include Adolfo Dominguez, David Valls, Jean Pierre Bua, Josep Abril and Kristia Robustella. An iconic Catalan name in the world of fashion is the dynamic Custo-Barcelona, whose flagship store is located in the shopping mall at Avinguda Diagonal 557.

Shopping Hours
Most shops open between 9am and 10am and close for lunch between 1 and 2pm, opening again between 4 and 5pm until 8pm. Many clothes and food shops close at 8.30 or 9pm. The large department stores, chain stores and shopping galleries remain open through lunch time. In the summer smaller shops may close on Saturday afternoon. Only bakeries, pastry shops and a few groceries are open on Sunday (until around 3pm).

High-Street Fashion

In the old town, Carrer de la Porta-ferrissa and Portal de l'Angel are good for young fashion stores. On and around Carrer d'Avinyó there are lots of trendy shops, such as Le Fortune and Cirkus, and El Born is a favourite spot for boutiques. El Raval is catching up fast: Caníbal, at Carrer del Carmé 5, has fun, one-off designs, while Carrer de la Riera Baixa is lined with vintage and second-hand clothes shops.

Shoes

These are great value. Look for Catalan and Spanish designers such as elegant Farrutx and Lotusse (contemporary classics), both found at Tascón (Passeig de Gràcia and El Born), and Camper (trendy, comfortable shoes) at Passeig de Gràcia and Carrer d'Elisabets in El Raval. For espadrilles try century-old La Manual Alpargatera at Carrer d'Avinyó 7. The best areas for shoes and bags are Portal de l'Angel, Rambla de Catalunya, Passeig de Gràcia and Diagonal.

FOOD

The best places to buy food are markets or *colmados* (grocer's shops). Look out for juicy marinated olives, sausages (chorizo and *sobrasada*), ham (*jabugo* is the best), cheese (Manchego, Mahon, Idiazabal), nuts, dried fruit, handmade chocolates, *turrón* (a nougat-type delicacy, available in hard or soft form), wine, cava and moscatel.

Some of the city's finest historic food stores include Casa Gispert (Carrer dels Sombrerers 23); Colmado Quilez (Rambla de Catalunya 63); chocolatiers Escribà (La Rambla 83); Fargas (Carrer del Pi 16), for excellent *turrón*; and Xocoa (Carrer de Petritxol 11), whose innovative chocolate flavours include 'five peppers' and 'thyme'.

Múrria (Carrer de Roger de Llúria 85) is home to an exquisite range, including own-label cava, in the prettiest of old Modernista interiors, while Planelles Donat (Portal de l'Angel 7) are specialists in *turrón* and delicious ice cream.

ENTERTAINMENT

Barcelona is one of the liveliest places in Europe. You will never be bored once the sun's gone down in the city that never sleeps, whether your preference be for clubs or bars, traditional or avant-garde music, film, dance or theatre.

Catalan Broadway
Avinguda Paral.lel in Poble Sec has long been associated with theatrical and musical productions. This main artery is being revived, and will provide an entertainment and gastronomic hub between Plaça d'Espanya and the port. The theatres, Apolo, Condal and Victoria, are on the route and the old music halls Artèria Paral.lel and El Molino have been restored. It is hoped that the Teatre Arnau will become a cultural centre.

Barcelona is hip, vibrant and buzzing, but it's not just about bars and all-night clubbing. This city is a multicultural melting pot, offering a variety of entertainment from traditional Catalan theatre to avant-garde dance and cutting-edge independent cinema. You can hang out with the cool crowd on the waterfront, listen to a top-class orchestra, or seek out traditional flamenco in an Old Town bar. There is strong government support for the arts, in particular for film and for those promoting Catalan identity and language.

THEATRE

Avinguda del Paral.lel was once regarded as Barcelona's theatre district and is now undergoing a revival *(see margin)*, although you will find theatres all over the city. Performances are often in Catalan but many theatres also host music and dance, which may have more appeal to non-Catalan speaking visitors.

Mainstream

Among the most popular theatres, showing a varied programme, is the Teatre Lliure *(see p.122)*; subtitles in English are provided for some shows. The Teatre Poliorama (La Rambla 115) stages comedy, musicals and theatre for

children. Other venues such as the L'Antic Teatre *(see p.122)* and Teatre Guasch (Carrer de Aragó 14) have programmes for all ages and tastes.

Catalan and Fringe

The most prominent of the theatres dedicated to the Catalan language is the government-funded Teatre Nacional de Catalunya *(see p.122)*, which also promotes dance. Fringe theatres include the inspiring Sala Beckett *(see p.122)* and avant-garde La Fura dels Baus (Carrer de Pujades 77–9). The open-air Teatre Grec in Montjuïc *(see p.76)* makes for an unusual summer experience.

MUSIC

Classical and Opera

In addition to the permanent venues, you will find performances in churches, museums and palaces. L'Auditori *(see p.63)* is home to the city's resident orchestra and hosts international and national names. Catalan and top international performers can be found in the glorious setting of the Palau de la Música Catalana *(see p.46)*. For opera fans the stunning Gran Teatre del Liceu *(see p.34)* is a must; internationally acclaimed singer, Montserrat Caballé was born in Barcelona and studied in the city.

Jazz, rock and pop

There is a strong tradition of jazz, and the Barcelona Jazz Festival (Oct–Dec), has taken place for over 40 years. Among the best places to hear jazz are the legendary Jamboree *(see p.34)* and the smaller, more intimate, Harlem Jazz Club *(see p.122)*.

The number of venues for music gigs is huge and you can catch some of the famous names from the world of rock and pop at big stadiums such as Camp Nou, Estadi Olímpic and the nearby Palau Sant Jordi arena. But there is also good local talent at smaller venues – try Razzmatazz *(see p.123)* for all genres of music. If you are here in early summer look out for the popular Sonar and Primavera music festivals.

DANCE

Barcelona's dance scene encompasses everything from ballet, tango and flamenco to a lively contemporary programme. Ballet and other dance forms can be seen at Teatre Lliure, Teatre Nacional and Gran Teatre del Liceu *(see opposite)*. Angel Corella brought his company, Ballet de Barcelona, to the city in 2012; it will be based in the Poble Nou development. For contemporary dance don't miss the innovative productions at the Teatre Mercat de les Flors *(see p.123)*.

FILM

Film is treated with reverence in Spain and Barcelona is no exception, playing host to several festivals during the year including those highlighting independent film and documentaries. Spain's most famous film-maker is Pedro Almodóvar, who has paid homage to Barcelona in film. His award-winning *All About My Mother* (1999) was shot almost entirely in the city. *Vicky Cristina Barcelona* (2008), directed by Woody Allen and starring Penélope Cruz, was also partly shot here.

Barcelona has the usual selection of big-screen cinemas showing the latest blockbusters (some in original language versions), plus an IMAX cinema at Port Vell. Government backing has meant that some good local, independent cinemas *(see p.123)* have survived.

NIGHTLIFE

On a first visit to Barcelona most people head down the busy La Rambla or mingle around Plaça Reial in the Barri Gòtic for the eclectic mix of bars, clubs and restaurants. Other districts offer distinct nightlife choices: El Born is the place to see and be seen, offering some of the most chic cocktails bars, while the popular El Raval is the most cosmopolitan and bohemian. The waterfront is a great place to be at night, too – a terrace at Port Vell, a bar in Barceloneta or at Port Olímpic with its many discos, bars and casino. For an alternative music scene try the up-and-coming Poble Nou district or head to Eixample, where students, local people and older night owls rub shoulders.

In the streets just to the west of here Gaixample can be found, a magnet for gay and lesbian clubbers.

Above from far left:
Palau de la Música Catalana; Bar Marsella in El Raval; flamenco; the music shop Casa Beethoven.

Flamenco
If you want to sample traditional flamenco try Los Tarantos *(see p.123)*; or for a full-blown show go to the more touristy El Tablao de Carmen at the Poble Espanyol in Montjuïc *(see p.77)*.

MODERNISME

Architecture is on the agenda of many visitors to Barcelona, due mainly to the outlandish works of Antoni Gaudí and his Modernista contemporaries. The city's defining architectural style looked to the past for its main influences.

Tragic End
A reclusive figure in his later years, Antoni Gaudí was run over by a tram in a street near the church while he was working on the Sagrada Família. Doctors were initially unable to identify the dishevelled old man who had been knocked over, thinking that he was a tramp. When it was finally discovered who he was, the entire city turned out for his funeral.

Modernisme is Barcelona's great contribution to architecture. Colourful and flamboyant, the architectural and artistic style emerged around the time of the Universal Exhibition, held in the Parc de la Ciutadella *(see p.61)*, in 1888 and continued until *c.*1930, thus corresponding to the Arts and Crafts and Art Nouveau (or Jugendstil, as it was known in Germany and Austria) movements in the rest of Europe. It shared with Arts and Crafts a focus on traditional styles and craftsmanship and, with Art Nouveau, a preoccupation with sinuous lines, organic form and ornament and a rebellion against rigid designs and colourless stone and plaster.

Catalan Renaissance

In Barcelona the new style assumed nationalist motifs and significance, which may be why it has been so carefully preserved. The movement was a part of the Catalan *Renaixença* (Renaissance), which looked to the past, taking on Catalan Gothic and its tradition of iron work, as well as acknowledging the highly elaborate styles of Islamic Spain.

The city's 19th-century expansion (the Eixample) gave architects the freedom and space to experiment, and this area is where the majority of the city's Modernista buildings are located *(see p.68)*.

KEY FIGURES

The movement's greatest practitioners were Antoni Gaudí i Cornet (1852–1926), Lluís Domènech i Montaner (1850–1923), a professor of Barcelona University's School of Architecture, and one of his pupils, Josep Puig i Cadafalch (1867–1957). At the Universal Exhibition Domènech designed what is now the Laboratori de Natura (the former Museu Zoologia, *see p.61),* based on Valencia's red-brick Gothic Stock Exchange, which afterwards became a workshop for ceramics, wrought iron and glass-making. Furnishings and details were an essential ingredient in Modernista buildings, in the same way that a coherent design was key to Arts and Crafts and Art Nouveau design. In the years immediately following its heyday, Modernisme was considered the epitome of bad taste, but the pendulum has swung back again, and Modernista buildings have become symbols of a vibrant city.

HIGHLIGHTS

Illa de la Discòrdia

The best starting point to understand Modernisme is the 'block of discord', three neighbouring buildings in Passeig de Gràcia. The block gained its name because of the close juxtaposi-

tion of three outstanding buildings – Domènech's Casa Lléo Morera, Puig's Casa Amatller and Gaudí's Casa Batlló *(see p.69)* – each of which is in a conflicting style, although they are all categorised as Modernista.

Gaudí Buildings

Having worked under Josep Fontseré on the Parc de la Ciutadella and the Plaça del Rei *(see pp.61 and 40)*, Gaudí earned his first commission, the Casa Vicens *(see p.84)* in Gràcia, aged 32. In 1878 he met wealthy textile manufacturer Count Eusebi Güell, whose fortune and passion for experimental architecture – and his ability to accept the architect's wildly imaginative ideas – were crucial to Gaudí's rising star. It led to the building, from 1886–8, of the Palau Güell *(see p.55)* and, later, from 1900, the Park Güell *(see p.73)*.

Gaudí's other key buildings include La Pedrera *(see p.70)*, on which he worked from 1905, Casa Batlló *(see above)* and the monumental Sagrada Família *(see p.72)*, on which he worked from 1883; the deeply religious architect was still designing the church, with its extravagant organic lines, when he died aged 74 in 1926 *(see margin, left)*.

Other Key Works

Other key Modernista works include the Unesco-protected Palau de la Música Catalana *(see p.46)*, an extraordinarily sumptuous building, with a spectacular interior. Its facade, crowded with sculptures and dazzling mosaics, is rather cramped down Carrer de Sant

Francesc de Paula. There are daily tours of the building, but it is best to attend a concert beneath the stained-glass dome that suffuses the auditorium with a mellow light.

Hospital de la Santa Creu i Sant Pau *(see p.73)*, designed by Domènech, was the most advanced in Europe when it was completed in 1901. It is essentially a series of pavilions connected by underground tunnels and is one of the Modernista highlights of the city. Also by Domènech, at Carrer de Mallorca 291, is Casa Thomas, built for the engraving business of a relative. The top three storeys and the protruding gallery on the top storey were added by his son-in-law, Francesc Guàrdia.

Key works by Puig i Cadafalch include the Casaramona textile factory, at the foot of Montjuïc, which is now the vibrant CaixaForum cultural centre *(see p.77)*.

Above from far left: Hospital de la Santa Creu i de Sant Pau; Palau de la Música Catalana; stained glass at Casa Batlló; ironwork detail on the Palau Güell.

St George and the Dragon Catalonia's patron saint was a favourite Modernista theme. Gaudí's Casa Batlló is dedicated to the saint, with spiny dragons' 'bones' for window frames.

Below: sinuous bench, decorated with colourful Modernista *trencadis* (mosaic made from broken tiles) in Gaudí's Park Güell.

CATALAN

Visitors will quickly become aware that Catalan is the official language of Barcelona and Catalonia. Not only are all signs in Catalan, but Catalan is spoken among Barcelonans, even when in a group of non-Catalan speakers.

Catalan is a Romance language, meaning it is Latin based, a sister to Castilian (Spanish), French, Italian and Portuguese. It has a staccato quality that makes it sound very different from Castilian, though when written its similarities are more apparent.

EARLY USE

Catalan began to be used widely from the 13th century, particularly in legal codes, such as the *Consolat de Mar*, which laid down laws governing Mediterranean shipping. The four Great Chronicles describing the life of Jaume I (the Conqueror) are also from this time. One of the families who ended up in Mallorca as a result of Jaume's conquests was that of Ramón Lull (1232–1315), whose religious and philosophic writings in Catalan (as well as Latin and Arabic) were prodigious.

GOLDEN AGE

The Golden Age of Catalan literature was in the 15th century, when Jocs Florals (Floral Games) were introduced as linguistic competitions for troubadors. This was in imitation of similar events in Toulouse in France, where Languedocian, a regional language similar to Catalan, was spoken. *Tirant lo Blanc*, a

Usage
Catalan is spoken by at least 11 million people in Catalonia, Valencia, the Roussillon region of France, Andorra and some border areas of Aragón. It is also spoken in the Balearic Islands and the city of Alghero in Sardinia, both of which were ruled by Catalonia in the 13th to 14th centuries.

novel of chivalry written by Joanot Martorell and published in 1490, preceded Miguel de Cervantes' *Don Quixote* by over a century. Viewed by some as the greatest European novel of its century ('the best book of its kind in the world', says the priest in *Don Quixote*), *Tirant* has been translated worldwide.

18TH CENTURY

After the War of Succession (1705–15), Catalonia was punished for siding with the Habsburg Archduke Charles. Castilian became the official language, and Catalan was relegated to religious and popular use. It was not until the industrial revolution, and the emergence of a dynamic middle class during the 19th century, that an economic and cultural revival known as the *Renaixença* (Renaissance) enabled Catalan to recover as a vehicle of culture.

Its leading lights were poets, notably Jacint Verdaguer (1845–1902), a priest, who won many prizes in the Jocs Florals. His poetry is still required reading in schools, and his hymn *El Virolai* is sung daily by the choir at Montserrat monastery. The Catalan nationalist sentiment informed all the arts; Modernisme architecture, which harked back to the Golden Age, can be said to be a showpiece of Catalan aspiration.

20TH CENTURY

In 1907 the Institut d'Estudis Catalans was formed for 'the re-establishment and organisation of all things relating to Catalan culture'. When the Generalitat was set up in 1931, Catalan again enjoyed the status of official language.

However, Franco's victory in the Spanish Civil War (1936–9) stamped out Catalan. It was banned entirely from public use, as were Galician and Basque, the other regional languages of Spain. Books, newspapers and films were subjected to draconian censorship. The enforced implementation of an all-Castilian education system meant that a generation of Catalan speakers were unable to read or write their mother tongue, which they continued to use.

OFFICIAL LANGUAGE

With the recovery of democracy in Spain, Catalan was established alongside Castilian as the official language of Catalonia. Campaigns were launched, and staunch nationalists made their views felt. It was not an easy time: many people in the city are not native Catalans and were worried that their children would be taught in a language they did not understand. But the government set about implementing a policy of 'linguistic normalisation', whereby Catalan was reinstated in all aspects of public life, government and the media. In 1990 the European Parliament passed a resolution recognising Catalan and its use in the European Union, and there was even a move to send a separate Catalan national team to the 1992 Olympics.

Nowdays, Catalan thrives in the arts and sciences, the media and advertising. Barcelona is a bilingual city, although varying degrees of proficiency in the different languages are evident. Some older people, educated before the Civil War, may have an imperfect knowledge of Castilian, and, while Catalan is almost universally understood, older immigrants from elsewhere in Spain may not speak it. People schooled during the past two decades are generally proficient in both languages.

Foreign films shown in the city are increasingly being dubbed into Catalan. The surge in nationalism was highlighted when the centre-right Nationalist Party (CiU) won overall control in Barcelona and Girona in municipal elections in 2011 and Xavier Trias became mayor, the first time a Catalan nationalist has held the post.

Above from far left: signs in Catalan.

Shops/Museums
Open *Obert*
Closed *Tancat*
Monday *Dilluns*
Tuesday *Dimarts*
Wednesday *Mimecres*
Thursday *Dijous*
Friday *Divendres*
Saturday *Dissabetes*
Sunday *Diumenge*

Useful Phrases

Good morning *Bon dia*
Good afternoon/evening *Bona tarda*
Good night *Bona nit*
How are you? *Com està vostè?*
Very well thanks, and you? *Molt bé, gràcies i vostè?*
Goodbye, see you again *Adéu, a reveure*
What's your name? *Com us diu?*
My name is… *Em dic…*
Where is the toilet please? *On és el lavabo, sisplau?*
Do you accept credit cards? *Accepteu targes de credit?*
1–10: *U/un/una, dos/dues, tres, quatre, cinc, sis, set, vuit, nou, deu*

HISTORY: KEY DATES

The city rose to power under Catalonia's medieval count-kings, then fell into decline and subject to the control of Madrid. The urge to break out of this inertia, and a deep Catalan identity, are key to Barcelona's inventive energy.

Did You Know?
In 1836, the first steamship rolled off a slipway in Barceloneta; gaslight was introduced in 1842; and in 1848 Spain's first railway linked Barcelona to Mataró, some 30km (19 miles) north.

Ramón Casas
Casas (1866–1932) was one of the most representative of the Modernista artists who flourished in the late 19th century in Barcelona. Above are his self-portrait on a tandem, painted for the café Els Quatre Gats *(see p.37)* and a portrait of a woman.

EARLY HISTORY TO THE GOLDEN AGE

237 BC	The Carthaginian Hamilcar Barca makes a base at Barcino.
206 BC	The Romans defeat the Carthaginians.
AD 531–54	Barcelona is made capital of the Visigoths.
711	Moorish invasion of Spain; they remain until 1492.
878	Wilfred (Guifré) the Hairy founds dynasty of counts of Barcelona.
1096–1131	Ramón Berenguer III extends the Catalan empire.
1213–76	Jaume I consolidates the empire, and expands Barcelona.
1359	The Corts Catalanes (Parliament of Catalonia) is established. The 14th century is the Golden Age of Catalonia.
1395	The Jocs Florals – annual competitions for poets and troubadors – are initiated in Catalonia.

IMPERIAL SPAIN

1469	Ferdinand and Isabella unite Aragón and Castile.
1494	The administration of Catalonia is put under Castilian control.
1516	Carlos I (Charles V, Holy Roman Emperor) takes the throne.
1659	Catalan territories north of the Pyrenees are ceded to France.
1701–13	War of Spanish Succession.
1713–14	Siege of Barcelona by Felipe V's forces; Ciutadella fortress built.
1835	Convents are disbanded by government decree; many are pulled down to give way to such new buildings as the Liceu and Boqueria.
1860	The building of the Eixample, designed by Ildefons Cerdà, begins.
1883	Antoni Gaudí begins work on the Sagrada Família.

THE MODERN ERA

1888	Barcelona hosts its first Universal Exhibition.
1897	The café Els Quatre Gats opens and becomes a haunt of artists and writers. Picasso, aged 19, exhibits here for the first time.
1914	The Mancomunitat (provincial government) is formed in Catalonia.

1923	General Primo de Rivera sets up a dictatorship and bans Catalan.
1929	A second Universal Exhibition is held, in the grounds of Montjuïc. Buildings including the Poble Espanyol are constructed.
1931	The Republican party comes to power.
1932	Catalonia is granted a short-lived statute of independence.
1936–9	Civil War ends in Franco's rule and isolates Spain. The Catalan language and the expression of Catalan customs are banned.
1975	Franco dies, and Juan Carlos is made king. Catalan is recognised as an official language.
1979	Statute of Autonomy; Catalan is restored as an official language.
1980	Jordi Pujol becomes president of Catalonia.
1986	Spain joins European Community (European Union). A wave of building begins in preparation for the Olympics.
1992	The Olympic Games are held in Barcelona.
1994	The Liceu opera house is devastated by fire.

21ST CENTURY

2003	Pujol is replaced as president of Catalonia by Pasqual Maragall.
2004	The city extends north, around Diagonal Mar, for Forum 2004.
2006	A new Catalan statute is passed. Jordi Hereu becomes the third socialist mayor of the city. Maragall stands down, and is replaced by José Montilla as president.
2010	The Sagrada Família is consecrated by Pope Benedict XVI.
2011	Xavier Trias of the Catalan Nationalist party (CiU) is elected mayor in July, ending 32 years of socialist leadership.

Above from far left: depiction of 13th-century *Assault on the City of Mallorca*, in the Palau Nacional; Barcelona falls to the armies of Felipe V, 11 September 1714.

Commemorations and Celebrations
The year 1992 was not just an important date for Barcelona because of the Olympics. It was also the 500th anniversary of Columbus's discovery of America and the expulsion of the Moors from Spain. It was not until 1493 that Columbus – Cristobal Colom – returned in triumph to Barcelona, to be received by Ferdinand and Isabella in the Saló de Tinell in the Royal Palace. The Genoese navigator, whose statue stands on a plinth at the foot of La Rambla, did Barcelona little good with his discovery. Seville was the city granted the right to trade with the New World, and Barcelona suffered economic decline.

Left: poster advertising the Barcelona Universal Exhibition in 1929.

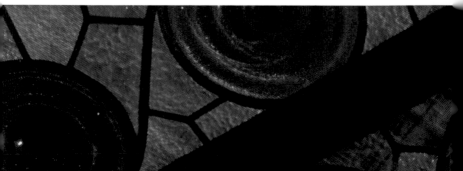

WALKS AND TOURS

LA RAMBLA

One of the world's most attractive avenues, La Rambla is the first place any visitor to Barcelona should head for. Animated day and night, it always has something worth seeing – even if it is just the passers-by.

DISTANCE 1.5km (1 mile)	
TIME 1½ hours	
START Plaça de Catalunya	
END Port Vell	
POINTS TO NOTE	

This is an easy stroll that can be done at any time of day. Unfortunately, you need to be on your guard against pickpockets on this popular stretch.

This leafy pedestrian avenue was once a river running beside the old city wall to the sea. On the left as you head down to the port is the Ciutat Vella, the Old Town, with tempting lanes and alleys *(see pp.36 and 42)*, while signs to the modern Museu d'Art Contemporani (MACBA) and Casa Güell, the only Gaudí building in this area, beckon on the right (southwest), in the old working-class Raval district *(see p.52)*. Traffic rumbles over the cobbles either side of the wide, plane-tree shaded promenade, and you will cross back and forth, as sights and attractions entice.

PLAÇA DE CATALUNYA

At the top of La Rambla is the **Plaça de Catalunya ❶**, where the Old Town ends and the new city (the Eixample, *see p.68*), laid out during the early 20th century and extending inland, begins. A pavement star in the middle of this large open square marks the geographical heart of the city.

The 1925 El Corte Inglés (The English Style) department store is on the northeast side of the square. The airport bus stops beside it, and nearby is the 'i' sign of the underground **tourist information** centre. An angular monument by local sculptor Josep María Subirachs commemorates Francesc

Below: bird's-eye view of the Rambla.

Macià (1859–1933), president of the Generalitat before the Civil War. Chess players tend to gather nearby. Flanking the square to the southwest is the popular **Café Zurich,** see ⑪①.

LA RAMBLA

From here the **Rambla** (from the verb *ramblar*, meaning to stroll) begins, a 1.2km (1-mile) promenade of colourful stalls selling such items as birds, flowers, newspapers and magazines, with pavement cafés sheltered beneath its established plane trees. Musicians, mime artists, tango dancers, fire eaters, fortune tellers and other entertainers add to the diversion day and night.

A fashionable place to stroll since the 19th century, La Rambla is in fact made up of five different *rambles*: Canaletes, Estudis, Sant Josep, Caputxins and Santa Mònica, the last three taking their names from convents that lined the southwest (right-hand) side of the street, giving it the name of 'Convent Way'. In the 1830s these powerful institutions were

Food and Drink 🍴

① CAFÉ ZURICH

Plaça de Catalunya; tel: 93 317 91 53; daily 8am–11pm; €

This city institution was rebuilt as part of El Triangle commercial centre, when the city was propelled into the 20th century for the 1992 Olympic Games. Slow down at its pavement tables, which spill onto the square, and choose from café standards of sandwiches, salads, etc., plus delicious pastries and coffee.

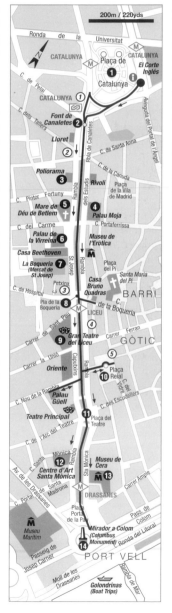

Above from far left: the *modernista* pharmacy Nadal; statue on the Plaça de Catalunya; perfume bottles in the Triangle shopping centre; mid-19th-century ironwork on La Rambla.

Above: flowers, street performer and fresh fruit on the Rambla.

Underground Hub
Plaça de Catalunya is the city's main transport hub, with a warren of underground passages leading to both FGC trains (for the suburbs) and national Renfe trains; several metro lines also stop here.

City Gates

The four city gates that gave access into the Old Town from La Rambla were at Santa Ana, La Boqueria, Portaferrissa and Drassanes. An attractive tiled fountain (*illustrated above*) in Carrer de la Portaferrissa shows how they once looked.

Below: Casa Beethoven's *raison d'être* in lights.

reduced by riots and reforms. Until the 15th century, the city wall ran down the southwestern side of the avenue.

Top of the Avenue

The first section, **Rambla de Canaletes**, takes its name from the 19th-century **Font de Canaletes ❷** drinking fountain, now a popular meeting place. Jubilant Barça fans traditionally gather here to celebrate their team's victories. The story goes that if you drink from the fountain's waters, you are sure to return to Barcelona. If, however, you would prefer a taste of something less puritanical, make a brief detour left into Carrer dels Tallers, for **Boadas**, see ⑪②.

Back on the main street, the next stretch is the **Rambla dels Estudis**, named after the university that was here until 1714. At No. 115, on the right, is **Poliorama ❸** (tel: 93 317 75 99; www.

teatrepoliorama.com), a 64-seat theatre, where comedies and musicals are the mainstay. Its upper floors house the Royal Academy of Sciences and Arts. Look up to see the city's first clock, erected in 1888 and inscribed *Hora Oficial* (Official Time).

Palau Moja

Opposite, beyond the Hotel Rivoli, is the colonnade of the bookshop of the Generalitat (Catalonia's autonomous government), which has maps and lavish books on the city and region. The shop occupies part of the ground floor of the 18th-century, neoclassical **Palau Moja ❹** (Carrer de la Portaferrissa 1; tel: 93 316 27 40; call ahead to arrange a visit; free), belonging to the Generalitat's Department of Culture. It hosts temporary exhibitions and is worth dipping into to see the fine first-floor Grand Salon's Baroque murals by Francesc Pla (1743–92). The main entrance to the palace, and to the courtyard, is in Carrer de la Portaferrissa, once one of the main alleys into the Old Town. Today the lively shopping street is popular for shoes, fashion and leather goods.

Mare de Déu de Betlem

Opposite the palace across La Rambla is the **Mare de Déu de Betlem ❺** (Carrer del Carme 2; tel: 93 318 38 23; free), a 17th-century Baroque church, bare since being burnt out in the Civil War and only recently renovated. This was part of a Jesuit convent, and a statue of the order's founder, the Basque-born saint, Ignatius Loyola, is joined by St Boromeu to flank the entrance. Since

Food and Drink 🍴

② BOADAS

Carrer dels Tallers 1; tel: 93 318 95 92; Mon–Sat noon–3pm, 6pm–2am; €

Barcelona's oldest cocktail bar, with 1930s decor and caricatures of the original owner. He mixed a mean *mojito*, a skill learned from his Cuban parents; his daughter, Dolors, continues the tradition.

③ PASTILERIA ESCRIBÀ

Rambla de les Flores 83; tel: 93 301 60 27; Mon–Thur noon–5pm, 8–11pm, Sat–Sun noon–5pm; €

Just one outlet of the famous Escribà patisserie and chocolate makers, with fare as enchanting as its facade.

1963 the church has staged charming displays of carefully crafted nativity scenes *(pessebres)*, from mid-November until February.

Palau de la Virreina

Beyond the church, the pavement is set back to give a grand vista of the **Palau de la Virreina** ❻ (La Rambla 99; tel: 93 316 10 00; www.virreina.bcn.cat; Tue–Sun noon–8pm; free), an imposing rococo building with lavish masonry and metalwork decoration. It was completed in 1777 for Manuel Amat, Spain's pleasure-loving viceroy to Peru, but he died shortly after taking up residence. His widow lived here for many years hence the name: 'Palace of the Viceroy's Wife'.

Built around two courtyards, it is now called the Virreina Centre de la Imatge, and partially open as a centre for cultural events and major exhibitions. At the front of the building is a box office for events in the city.

Beside the palace is the dinky Modernista **Casa Beethoven**, which has been selling sheet music since 1920. On the other side of the street, at No. 96, the first-floor **Museu de l'Eròtica** (tel: 93 318 98 65; www.erotica-museum.com; daily June–Sept 10am–9pm, Oct–May 10am–8pm; charge) showcases saucy artworks, photographs and sculptures, etc.

La Boqueria

The 19th-century Mercat de Sant Josep, better known as **La Boqueria** ❼ (www.boqueria.info; Mon–Sat 8am–8.30pm), is named after the convent that stood just past the Palau de la Virreina. Here, top restaurateurs and other gourmets do their early-morning shopping. Look out for fungi in season, super-fresh vegetables and fruit, delectable ranges of olives, cheeses and nuts, butchers' stalls selling all you need for nose-to-tail eating, plus seafood glistening on ice.

Just beyond the market on the corner of Carrer Petxina is an attractive mosaic-fronted Modernista shop, the **Antigua Casa Figueras**. It now houses the **Pastileria Escribà**, see ⓣⓘ③, owned by the Barcelona chocolate-producing dynasty, the Escribà family.

Breakfast at La Boqueria

The market is a great place to eat at any time of the day, but for a special experience come early for an *esmorçar de cullera*, a hearty breakfast. The 18-seater Quim de la Boqueria is where local foodies gather from 7am for breakfast prepared by Quim Márquez, whose innovative dishes include *fricassée* of artichokes and white asparagus, fried egg with sautéed mushrooms topped with caramel foie, and tiny clams steamed in sparkling wine. Pinotxo, open from 6am, is a lively market tapas bar specialising in Catalan cuisine, and there is always a warm welcome here from the Bayen family. Alternatively, try the equally busy Kiosk Universal.

Musical Favourites
Catalonia has produced several major opera stars, among them Victoria de los Angeles, Montserrat Caballé and José Carreras, as well as such outstanding musicians as pianist and composer Isaac Albéniz, cellist Pau Casals (who was famously proud of his Catalonian birth, frequently performing *El Cant del Ocells – The Song of the Birds* – a haunting Catalan folk song); and the composer Federico Mompou.

Pla de la Boqueria

In front of the market is the square of the same name, **Pla de la Boqueria ❽**. At the point where it breaks up the line of trees, lanes on the left lead into the Barri Gòtic *(see p.36)*. Pla de la Boqueria was once the place of public executions. Nowadays, it is a considerably more pleasant place, enlivened by a colourful mosaic pavement by Joan Miró.

Beside it is **Casa Bruno Quadras**, built in the Oriental style, decorated with fans, lanterns and an elaborate coiling green Chinese dragon by Josep Vilaseca. It was originally designed to house an umbrella shop in the mid-1880s, but now shelters a savings bank.

Gran Teatre del Liceu

The block from Carrer de Sant Pau to Carrer de la Unió is taken up by the

Gran Teatre del Liceu ❾ (bookings
tel: 93 485 99 13; www.liceubarcelona.cat; tours daily 10am–1pm; charge). The limited facilities inside this classic, plush 19th-century opera house were improved when the building was reconstructed following a major fire in 1994. One of the city's great institutions, it attracts world-renowned opera stars and also hosts jazz, cabaret and film (including some free entertainment in the foyer). There is a shop and café in the basement, though the historic **Café de l'Opera**, see ⑪④, opened in 1929 and one of the few remaining traditional cafés in the city, is just on the other side of La Rambla.

Vintage Hotels

Many historic hotels line La Rambla, among them the **Oriente** *(see p.112)*, just beyond the Liceu. The interior cloister of the Franciscan college on which it was built, remains intact.

The first turning on the right after the Oriente is **Carrer Nou de la Rambla**, housing, just along on the left, at Nos 3–5, **Palau Güell** *(see p.55)*, the only building by Gaudí in the Old Town.

Plaça Reial

Opposite Carrer Nou de la Rambla, a faded grand arch leads into the **Plaça Reial ❿**, one of the city's liveliest squares. Beneath its colonnades are cafés and tapas restaurants such as **Les Quinze Nits**, see ⑪⑤. At No. 17 is legendary jazz club, **Jamboree** (tel: 93 319 17 89; www.masimas.com; daily 8pm–11am; charge), which has been here since the 1960s. Top jazz musicians

---

Food and Drink 🍴

④ CAFÉ DE L'OPERA
La Rambla 74; tel: 93 317 75 85; www.cafeoperabcn.com; daily 8.30am–2.30am; €€
Open all day long, this historic café with old-time waiters, consummate professionals in traditional attire, is an ideal choice for a break at any time of day. It does good breakfasts, and is a favourite pit stop among the opera crowd after a performance.

⑤ LES QUINZE NITS
Plaça Reial 6; tel: 93 317 30 75; daily 1–3.45pm, 8.30–11.30pm; €€
This popular restaurant, serving Mediterranean cuisine, is well situated in the Plaça Reial. It is a good spot for a meal at any time, but the inexpensive set lunch menu is particularly good value.

perform in its intimate vaulted basement and it also hosts club nights and Latin, funk, soul and hip-hop acts.

Towards the Port

After the Plaça Reial, the Rambla opens up on the left into **Plaça del Teatre** ⓫, where portrait artists ply their trade and old men sit for hours over coffee in a traditional café. Barcelona's first theatre was on this site, and Frederic Soler (1835–95), founder of its present incarnation, the **Teatre Principal**, is commemorated in an imposing statue. He is unfortunately best known these days because a public toilet has been built beneath the statue – a great relief (literally), as bars are increasingly unwelcoming to non-clients using their facilities.

Further down, at La Rambla 7, on the right, is the **Centre d'Art Santa Mònica** ⓬ (tel: 93 567 11 10; www. artssantamonica.cat; Tue–Fri 11am–9pm, Sat 11am–2pm, 4pm–9pm; free). The former cloisters have been converted into three storeys of open gallery space, mostly for art installations. The second-floor bar and café have a substantial terrace with views over the Rambla. A cultural information centre is on the ground floor.

The old-fashioned green ticket booth in the middle of La Rambla sells tickets for the **Museu de Cera** ⓭ (Wax Museum; Passatge de la Banca; tel: 93 317 26 49; www.museoceracbn.com; summer daily 10am–10pm, winter Mon–Fri 10am–1.30pm, 4–7.30pm, Sat–Sun 11am–2pm, 4.30–8.30pm; charge). More than 360 waxworks of mainly Spanish personalities appear in this handsome former bank. Also inside is the café El Bosc de les Fades, an enchanted 'forest' with magically lit gnarled trees and gnomes.

Mirador a Colom

You can't miss the 50m (165-ft) high **Mirador a Colom** ⓮ (Columbus Monument; tel: 93 302 52 24; daily 10am–8.30pm; charge), designed by Gaietà Buïgas, with a crowning sculpture of Columbus by Rafael Arché, for the Universal Exhibition of 1888. Note that Columbus is not pointing towards the New World, as intended; locals claim that he is simply pointing to the sea. For a great view of the port and the city, take the elevator to the top.

Just south of the statue is the seafront and **Port Vell**, where the Rambla turns into the **Rambla de Mar** *(see p.56)*, a walkway over to the marina.

Above from far left: inside the Liceu opera house; José Carreras and Montserrat Caballé; shopping on the Rambla; Oriental dragon and fan on Casa Bruno Quadras.

Pipa Club
From 6pm daily smokers can enjoy unrestricted puffs at the Pipa Club (Plaça Reial 3; tel: 93 302 47 32; www.bpipa club.com). It has a number of rooms and a Victorian, clubby atmosphere, and serves food. It also puts on occasional live jazz.

Below: city bikes by the port.

ROYAL BARRI GÒTIC

The complex comprising the cathedral and royal palace is at the heart of the Old Town, which also incorporates a chunk of Roman Barcino. These imposing constructions contrast with the area's delicate cloisters and narrow lanes.

DISTANCE 1.5km (1 mile)

TIME 3–4 hours

START Avinguda del Portal de l'Angel

END Plaça del Rei

POINTS TO NOTE

This is an easy stroll through the pedestrianised streets of one of the most complete medieval quarters in Europe. Note that these lanes tend to be very busy on Saturdays.

This walk starts at the bottom of Plaça de Catalunya, once the location of the Portal de l'Angel, the main inland gate into the medieval city. It can be combined with elements of the following walk, covering the 'Official Barri Gòtic', *(see p.42)*.

AVINGUDA DEL PORTAL DE L'ANGEL

The busy **Avinguda del Portal de l'Angel** ❶ leads into the Barri Gòtic from the Plaça de Catalunya. This wide shopping thoroughfare is ideal if you are hunting for shoes or moderately priced fashion.

Santa Anna

Iron gates halfway down the first turning on the right, **Carrer de Santa Anna**, lead to the two-tiered Gothic cloisters of the medieval church of **Santa Anna** ❷ (Mon–Sat 9am–1pm, 6.30–8pm, feast days 10am–2pm; free). Built for the Knights Templar in the 12th century, the church's cloister and chapter house are still intact.

The Necropolis

From Santa Anna go down Carrer de Bertrellans, opposite the wonderful fan shop Guantería Alonso, into **Plaça de la Vila de Madrid** ❸, which has been

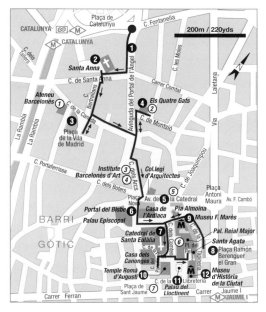

modelled to show off a Roman necropolis, discovered in the 1950s. However, it is rather overpowered by the large Decathlon sports store, which dominates the square.

Opposite, at Carrer de la Canuda 6, is a palatial 18th-century mansion that houses the **Ateneu Barcelonès** cultural centre. Inside are fine paintings by Francesc Pla. It holds temporary exhibitions and has a good restaurant, **Ateneu**, see ⑪①, and an attractive garden.

Els Quatre Gats

Return to Avinguda del Portal de l'Angel and just back up the street on the far side is Carrer de Montsió, where tucked away is Casa Martí, a fine Modernista building designed in 1897 by architect Puig i Cadafalch. It is famous as **Els Quatre Gats ❹** (The Four Cats), see ⑪②, an arty café frequented by Barcelona's artists around the start of the 20th century.

Art Colleges

Continue down Avinguda del Portal de l'Angel, and as you take a left fork into Carrer dels Arcs, you will see the restored Modernista Hotel Catalonia Catedral at No. 10, where you can pause for a relaxing lunch, see ⑪③. Continue to the **Institute Barcelonès d'Art**, home of the Reial Cercle Artístic, which has a restaurant, see ⑪④ *(p.39)*, and exhibition space.

Beyond it on the left is the **Col.legi d'Arquitectes**, the facade surmounted by a frieze designed by Picasso and executed by the Norwegian artist Carl Nesjar. Reminiscent of cave drawings

and completed in 1961, it was Picasso's first work to appear in Spain since his self-imposed exile after the Civil War.

ROMAN GATES

The lane now opens out on to **Avinguda de la Catedral ❺**. The Roman wall that encircled the 4th-century city begins its surviving 1.5km (1-mile) stretch here. The wall, constructed using

Above from far left:
the area's atmospheric alleyways; the Casa de l'Ardiaca *(see p.38)*.

Brilliant Barcelona
At the end of the 16th century, writer Lope de Vega wrote, 'Just as a splendid facade enhances the value of a building, so great Barcelona stands at the entrance to Spain, like a portico framing a famous threshold.'

Below: details of Picasso's frieze (executed by Carl Nesjar) above the Col.legi d'Arquitectes.

Food and Drink 🍴

① ATENEU
Carrer de la Canuda 6; tel: 93 318 52 38; www.ateneugastronomic. com; Mon 10am–6.30pm, Tue–Sat 10.30am–12.30am; €€
The restaurant in the Ateneu Barcelonès cultural centre, beside Plaça de la Vila de Madrid, serves hearty Catalan farmyard favourites including duck, goose and rabbit.

② ELS QUATRE GATS
Carrer de Montsió 3; tel: 93 302 41 40; www.4gats.com; daily 10am–1am; €€
In this historic arts café and restaurant, 19-year-old Pablo Picasso had his first exhibition in 1900. It is very touristy, but still worth a visit: the food is very acceptable and the sense of place is a big pull.

③ LA BRASSERIE DU GOTHIQUE
Hotel Catalonia Catedral, Carrer dels Arcs; tel: 93 330 03 03; www.brasserie-gothique.com; daily 1–4pm, 8–11pm; €€
If you are here at lunch time this French hotel restaurant is a calm retreat from the busy tourist area. Choose from a menu that includes duck cannelloni, scallops and fondues. Seating inside and out.

Rooftop View

For a good view of the Barri Gòtic and a close-up of the spires, take the elevator from the nave (to the left of the entrance) to the roof of the cathedral. It is well worth a few euros for the view.

Above: the famously bad-tempered cathedral geese.

colossal stones, the largest of which is some 3.5m (12ft) thick and 9.5m (30ft) high, originally had 78 square towers, of which several remain.

One tower forms the **Portal del Bisbe ❻**, beside which you can see remains of the aqueduct that brought water to the Roman city. Through this 'gate' on the right is the **Palau Episcopal** (Bishops' Palace; tel: 93 270 10 12), built in 1769 around the 12th-century courtyard, which is visible through the main entrance.

The interiors of three other Roman towers can be seen in the **Casa de l'Ardiaca** (Archdeacon's House; tel: 93 318 11 95; free), next to the cathedral. The house has an attractive patio, where a palm tree towers over a fountain. Note the letter box decorated with swallows and tortoises – signifying swift and slow mail – added in 1908

by Modernista architect Domènech i Montaner. Facing the Casa de l'Ardiaca is the atmospheric Romanesque chapel of **Santa Eulàlia**, built in 1269 and one of the earliest parts of the cathedral, which it adjoins.

CATEDRAL DE SANTA EULÀLIA

There has been a Christian church on Plaça de la Seu, the site of the present cathedral, since the 10th century. The first was destroyed by Al-Mansur, vizier of Córdoba, in AD985. The current **Catedral de Santa Eulàlia ❼** (tel: 93 342 82 60; www.catedralbcn.org; Mon–Fri 8am–12.45pm, 5–7.30pm, Sat until 6pm, Sun 8–9am, 5–6pm; cloister daily 9am–12.30pm, 5–7pm; free, charge for some areas) was begun in 1298 under Jaume II and completed in

Sunday Sardana

Every Sunday morning people gather outside the cathedral to dance Catalonia's traditional *sardana*. When the music starts, friends hold hands to form circles, placing any bags they are carrying in the centre of the ring. Anyone can join in simply by slipping in between two people – though not between a man and the woman on his right. When the circles grow too large, breakaway groups form new ones. The serious looks on the dancers' faces are the result of having to keep count of the short, sedate, steps and the bouncy long ones, so that everyone finishes exactly on cue. The accompanying band or *cobla*, has 11 players, and the leader, seated, plays a *flabiol* (three-holed flute) and taps the rhythm on a *tabal* strapped to his arm. Each tune lasts about 10 minutes and in an *audició*, a normal performance, there will be half a dozen tunes. The origins of the music date from the mid-19th century.

1417, though its main, west facade was not finished until the early 20th century. Long-term restoration means that scaffolding has become a permanent fixture.

Cathedral Interior and Cloisters

The austere, lofty cathedral has three naves and a central choir. Below the altar is the crypt of St Eulàlia, whose remains were placed here 1,000 years after she was martyred in the Roman purges of Dacian; her alabaster tomb, behind the altar, was carved in 1327. Of the 29 side chapels, the most notable is that of St Salvador, which features a *Transfiguration* (1442) by Bernat Martorell.

A plaque in the baptistery (left of the entrance), notes that the first six Carib Indians brought to Europe by Columbus were baptised here on 1 April 1493. In the Chapel of Christ Lepanto, (right of the entrance), is the crucifix borne in battle by the Christian flagship in the decisive Battle of Lepanto (1571), which defeated the Ottoman Turks.

Among the cathedral's highlights are its cloisters, which are enclosed by a 15th-century iron railing. The cool ambience is emphasised by the mossy Font de les Oques, a drinking fountain that takes its name from the 13 geese (one for every year that St Eulàlia lived) that reside here. Note on the floor the faint engraving of shoes and scissors reflecting the various guilds (of cobblers and tailors, etc.) that paid for the chapel.

Around the Cathedral

Opposite the cathedral is the **Hotel Colón**, see ⑪⑤. On the far side of the square, the Roman wall continues past the 15th-century almshouse, **Pia Almoina**, housing the **Museu Diocesa** (Avinguda de la Catedral 4; tel: 93 315 22 13; www.cultural. arqbcn.cat; Tue–Sat 10am–2pm, 5–8pm, Sun 11am– 2pm; charge), showcasing altarpieces, religious sculpture and other icons.

The wall then runs down Carrer de la Tapineria to **Plaça de Ramón Berenguer el Gran ❽**. The equestrian statue here, of the 12th-century count, who added the French region of Provence to Catalonia by marriage, is by Josep Llimona (1864–1934).

MUSEU FREDERIC MARÈS

To the left of the cathedral, Carrer dels Comtes leads down beside the complex of the former royal palace of the count-kings of Barcelona-Aragón. On the left, at Plaça de Sant Iu 5–6, is the **Museu Frederic Marès ❾** (tel: 93 256 35 00;

Above from far left: view from the cathedral roof; cathedral candles *(left)*, facade *(middle)* and lofty interior *(right)*.

Bargain Hunting
Every Thursday there is an antiques and bric-a-brac market in Plaça Nova outside the cathedral (10am–9pm, closed three to four weeks in August and early September).

Food and Drink

④ **REIAL CERCLE ARTÍSTIC**
Carrer dels Arcs 5; tel: 93 301 59 37; Mon 1–4pm, Tue–Sat 1–4pm, 8pm–midnight; € (lunch), €€ (dinner)
Treat yourself to a light lunch of cheese, pâté or salad on the terrace of this impressive palace or come back later for a more substantial dinner.

⑤ **HOTEL COLÓN**
Avinguda de la Catedral 7; tel: 93 301 14 04; www.hotelcolon.es; daily 1–3.30pm, 8–10.30pm; €€
This elegant, old-fashioned hotel has a good but expensive restaurant, Catedral, but you can also just sit at one of its pavement tables and enjoy a drink while watching the world go by.

Above from left: stonework *(left)*, tiles *(middle)* and icon *(right)* in the Museu Frederic Marès; Plaça del Rei.

Above: palm trees and lamp-posts by Gaudí, the architect's first public work, in the Plaça del Rei.

Below: Museu d'Història de la Ciutat.

www.museumares.bcn.es; Tue–Sat 10am–7pm, Sun 11am–8pm; charge, free first Sun in month). In the 13th century this was the bishop's palace, before becoming home to the counts of Barcelona and the count-kings of Barcelona-Aragón. It now houses an extraordinary collection of mainly religious artefacts brought together by Marès, a wealthy local sculptor who lived in the building and had a studio here until his death, at the age of 97, in 1991. There is a large Romanesque collection, with some particularly fine crucifixes, and even entire portals.

The ground and first floors house the sculpture collection. The Collector's Cabinet takes up the second and third floors, described as 'a museum within a museum'. Recent additions to the cabinet are the Weapons Hall and the Gentlemen's Hall. Memorabilia include toys, pipes and photographs, plus Marès' libary-studio. Sheltered in the courtyard is a pleasant café, see ⑪⑥.

TEMPLE ROMÀ D'AUGUSTI

Follow the cathedral's curving walls around Carrer de la Pietat, beside the 14th- to 16th-century **Casa dels Canonges**, and take the first left, Carrer del Paradis. Step inside the entrance of No. 7 to see four Corinthian columns that were part of the **Temple Romà d'Augusti ⑩** (Temple of Augustus; tel: 93 315 11 11; May–Oct Tue–Sat 10am–7pm, Sun 10am–8pm, Nov–Apr Tue–Sat 10am–5pm; free). Set on the highest point in the oppidum, this was the main religious building in Roman times and is now the city's largest single relic from that period.

PALAU DEL LLOCTINENT

Just beyond the Museu Frederic Marès a handsome doorway leads into the elegant courtyard of the **Palau del Lloctinent ⑪**, which takes its name from the Lloctinent (lord lieutenant), who resided here. Part of the former royal palace, and designed in Renaissance style from 1549–57 by Antoni Carbonell, the building was later embellished in Catalan-Gothic style, typified by horizontal lines and solid, plain walls (rather than lofty spaces, as in classic Gothic) between columns, octagonal towers and flat roofs.

PLAÇA DEL REI

Adjacent is the **Plaça del Rei**, the heart of the old royal city. The main royal buildings around the square are accessed through the excellent **Museu**

d'Història de la Ciutat **⑫** (City History Museum; Plaça del Rei 1; tel: 93 256 21 22; www.museuhistoria. bcn.es; Tue–Sat 10am–7pm, Sun 10am–8pm; charge includes admission to the former royal palace and chapel).

The museum occupies the 17th-century Casa Clariana-Padellàs, a merchant's house that was brought here, stone by stone, in 1930 after the nearby Via Laietana was driven through the Old Town. In the process of re-erecting the house, Roman remains were discovered beneath the ground, and now a huge area of the foundations of the Roman city has been opened up beneath the square. A lift takes visitors down to this subterranean city, which shows streets of shops and industries, from textile dyeing to wine-making.

These ancient stones also chart the development of the first Christian palace that stood here between the 6th and 8th centuries, prefiguring the palace of the Barcelona count-kings.

Palau Reial Major

Emerging from this Roman twilight, you arrive at the **Palau Reial Major**, the former royal palace, dominated by the **Saló del Tinell**, the great hall and throne room. Its enormous interior stone arches were designed in the 14th century for Pere III (the Ceremonious) by Guillem Carbonell, who was also responsible for much of the palace's facade. Columbus is said to have been received here by Ferdinand and Isabella. Today, it stages concerts and exhibitions.

The **Capella Reial de Santa Agata** (Royal Chapel of St Agatha), built for Jaume II (the Just) in 1312, features a rare embellishment in an otherwise rather austere complex. Jaume's coat of arms can be seen behind the retable of the Epiphany, painted by Jaume Huguet in 1464–5, while scenes of St Agatha's martyrdom are depicted in a chapel on the left.

ENDING THE WALK

Return to the front of the Museu d'Història de la Ciutat, where small quirky shops include, at No. 7, the candlemakers **Cereria Subirà**, the oldest shop in the city. Stop for a drink or a chocolate and *xurros* (*churros* – chunks of deep-fried batter coated in sugar) at the quaint **Mesón del Café**, see ⑪⑦. Alternatively, pick up a pastry from one of the *pastelerías* in this area: *tartaletas de music* ('music tarts' – sweet mixed-nut tartlets) or *empanadas catalanas* (pies filled with tuna and olives) are specialities.

Barcino Wine
Roman Barcino was known for its fish paste *(garum)* and inexpensive wine, Vi de le Laietanis, which travelled well – evidence of it has been found all over Europe. In Roman times, half to three-quarters of a litre (1–1½ pints) of wine was the daily intake.

Food and Drink 🍴

⑥ CAFE D'ESTIU
Plaça de Sant Iu 5–6; tel: 93 268 25 98; Apr–Sept Tue–Sun 10am–10pm; €
This shaded café in the courtyard outside the Museu Frederic Marès serves decent snacks. The name, meaning 'summer café', in Catalan, reflects the fact that it is open only from April to September.

⑦ MESÓN DEL CAFÉ
Carrer de la Llibreteria 16; tel: 93 315 07 54; Mon–Sat 7am–11pm; €
This quaint little café has been going since 1909. Perch on a bar stool for a delicious coffee or thick, rich hot chocolate and *xurros*.

OFFICIAL BARRI GÒTIC

This tour of the Gothic quarter centres on the government buildings on the area's main square, Plaça de Sant Jaume, and also takes in the Jewish quarter. In the surrounding streets you will find some of the city's most engaging old shops.

Above from left: rose window in Santa Maria del Pi; Catalan and Spanish flags on top of the Palau de la Generalitat, on Plaça de Sant Jaume, heart of the administrative part of the Barri Gòtic.

DISTANCE 2km (1¼ miles)

TIME 3–4 hours

START Pla de la Boqueria

END Carrer de Ferran/La Rambla

POINTS TO NOTE

It is easy to feel disorientated in the narrow streets of this quarter, but rest assured that you will never be far from Plaça de Sant Jaume on this roughly circular walk.

Halfway down La Rambla by the Liceu metro, the dragon on Casa Bruno Quadras *(see p.34)* on **Pla de la Boqueria ❶** marks the corner of Carrer del Cardenal Casañas. This lane of book- and print-sellers sets the tone for the walk and leads into one of the most characterful parts of the Barri Gòtic.

SANTA MARIA DEL PI

Among the highlights of the Barri Gòtic are **Plaça del Pi** and the adjacent **Plaça de Sant Josep Oriol**. Dominating both squares is the 14th-century Catalan-Gothic **Santa Maria del Pi ❷**, distinguished by its stained glass (including a fine rose window), much of it replaced after being destroyed in 1936 during the Civil War.

Plaça del Pi's handsome architecture includes the wonderful Modernista facade on La Gavineteria Roca, purveyors of cut-throat razors since 1911.

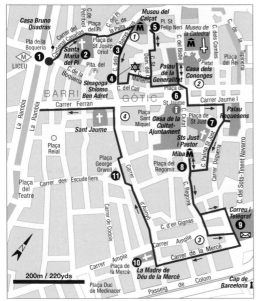

Food and Drink

① EL PORTALON

Carrer de Banys Nous 20; tel: 93 302 11 87; www.elportalonbcn.com; Mon–Sat 9am–midnight; €

This is a typical *bodega* with wine barrels and tapas. Offers good value and authentic ambience.

Carrers de Petritxol and de la Palla
In the northwest corner of Plaça del Pi is **Carrer de Petritxol**, a little street of art galleries and independent shops. Sala Parés, at No. 5, dates from 1845 and was the first gallery to exhibit work by Pablo Picasso. **Carrer de la Palla**, off Plaça de Sant Josep Oriol, is lined with antiques stores (with the focus on tiles and ceramics) and bookshops, such as Angel Batlle, at No. 23, which also has a wide selection of old prints.

Carrer de Banys Nous
Halfway up the street, take a right turn down **Carrer de Banys Nous ❸**, a delightful street with further antiques stores and bric-a-brac sellers. There is also an atmospheric bodega, **El Portalon**, see ⑪①, a cosy *granja (see margin, right)* at No. 4, and, at No. 11, Artesania Catalunya, home to crafts workshops. At the end of the street, on the corner of Carrer del Call, is the hat shop Sombrererìa Orbach, selling Borsolinos and genuine Catalan berets.

JEWISH QUARTER

The narrow, sunless lanes between Plaça del Pi and Plaça de Sant Jaume are redolent of medieval Barcelona. Here, the pleasure is simply in walking the streets, peering into patios, window shopping, menu reading and wondering at the history heaped up behind walls of solid stone.

Much of this area was the *call*, or Jewish quarter – the word comes from the Hebrew *qahqal*, meaning 'meeting' – with a large Jewish population here from the 12th century until 1391. That year, following widescale rioting in the wake of accusations that the Jews had brought the plague to Spain, the *call* was virtually destroyed, many of its residents murdered, and the rest given the choice of conversion or expulsion. A century later all non-Catholic religions were banned altogether.

The Synagogue
Turn left into Carrer del Call, then first left and first right into Carrer Marlet. Set within the wall of No. 1 is a Hebrew memorial stone, which dates to 1314 and reads simply, 'Holy foundation of Rabbi Samuel Hassardi for whom life never ends. Year 62'.

At No. 5 is the restored medieval **Sinagoga Shlomo Ben Adret ❹** (tel: 93 317 07 90; www.calldebarcelona.org; Mon–Fri 11am–5.30pm, Sat–Sun 11am–3pm; charge), once the largest synagogue in the city.

Milk Stop
The Barri Gòtic is known for its *granges* (or *granjas*), literally 'dairies'. These traditional cafés sell mainly milk-based drinks, including *orxata*, a thick beverage made with milk and tiger nuts. *Granges* usually also have a good selection of pastries.

Below: one of many antiques shops in the Barri Gòtic.

Big Foot
An attraction in the Museu del Calçat is a huge pair of shoes made to fit the statue of Christopher Columbus *(see p.35)*, at the bottom of the Rambla. According to the *Guinness Book of Records*, these are the largest shoes in the world.

Museu del Calçat

Carrer Marlet leads into Carrer de Sant Domènec del Call, where you should turn left and stroll up to the attractive, shady **Plaça de Sant Felip Neri** ❺. At No. 5, once the location of the shoemakers' guild, is the **Museu del Calçat** (Museum of Footwear; tel: 93 301 45 33; Tue–Sun 11am–2pm; charge), which showcases the history of the craft from Roman times to the present day. Highlights include the largest shoe in the world *(see left)*.

Also overlooking Plaça de Sant Felip Neri is the chic Hotel Neri, housed in a lovely 18th-century mansion.

PLAÇA DE SANT JAUME

Carrer del Call emerges at the **Plaça de Sant Jaume** ❻, the administrative heart of the city, where the Roman Forum once stood. The square is a focal point for celebrations and also has a good place for a snack, see ⑪②.

Palau de la Generalitat

The left-hand side of the square is dominated by the imposing Gothic and Renaissance **Palau de la Generalitat** (tel: 93 402 46 00; wwwgencat.net; tours second and fourth Sun of month 10am–1.30pm; free), from where Catalonia is governed. It is topped by a statue of St George, the patron saint of Catalonia, and is decked with red roses (and opened to the public) on his saint's day: 23 April. The 15th-century chapel by Marc Safont and the first-floor **Patí dels Tarongers** (Orange Tree Patio) are among its highlights.

The lane leading up the right-hand side of the Generalitat is the Carrer del Bisbe. On the right is the 14th-century **Casa dels Canonges** (Canons' House), now Generalitat offices. A neo-Gothic bridge, based on the Venetian Bridge of Sighs, links the two buildings.

Ajuntament

Facing the Generalitat on Plaça de Sant Jaume is the **Ajuntament**, or Casa de la Ciutat, Barcelona's town hall (tel: 93 402 70 00; tours Sun 10am–1.30pm). The entrance is flanked by the figures of Jaume I and Joan Fiveller, a 15th-century councillor who established city freedoms. The building's two most notable rooms are the 14th-century Saló del Consell de Cent and the Saló de les Cròniques, where, in 1928, Josep Maria Sert painted scenes from the 14th-century Catalan expedition to Byzantium.

Food and Drink

② CONESA
Plaça de Sant Jaume 10; tel: 93 310 13 94; www.conesaentrepans.com; Mon–Sat 8.15am–10.15pm; €
A popular place on the corner of Carrer de la Libreteria and a good choice for their famously delicious, inexpensive hot sandwiches, with fillings including tortilla or ham and tomato.

③ EL TROPEZÓN
Carrer del Regomir 26; tel: 93 310 18 64; Thur–Tue noon–2am; €
Small, authentic tapas bar with a rustic feel and buzzing atmosphere; popular for its *patatas bravas* and *la bomba*, a potato croquette with chorizo, alioli and a spicy dipping sauce.

④ EL GRAN CAFÉ
Carrer d'Avinyó 9; tel: 93 318 79 86; www.restaurantelgrancafe.com; Sun–Thur 1pm–midnight, Fri–Sat 1pm–12.30am; €€€
This historic café, reminiscent of a classic Parisian Art Nouveau brasserie, has a handsome Modernista interior with huge chandeliers. Rather expensive but has a good-value set lunch.

There is a tourist information office on the ground floor.

SOUTH OF SANT JAUME

Go down Carrer de Jaume I, taking the second right into Carrer de Dagueria, where you can peek in at Casa Oliveras to see lacemakers at work. This lane leads into **Plaça de Sant Just ❼**, a quiet square overlooked by the church of **Sants Just i Pastor**.

An alley opposite leads down to **Palau Requesens**, home to the Reial Acadèmia de Bones Lletres, built against the **Roman wall**, which runs down Carrer del Sots-Tinent Navarro.

Head down Carrer de la Palma Sant Just and turn right at the bottom onto **Plaça del Regomir ❽**. On the left, note part of the Roman city's southern gate.

To the right, at Carrer de la Ciutat 4, is **Miba** (Museu d'idees i invents de Barcelona; tel: 93 332 79 30; www.mibamuseum.com; Mon–Fri 10am–7pm, Sat until 8pm, Sun 10am–2pm; charge), a modern museum, dedicated to ideas, inventions and creativity, which opened in 2011.

Continue down Carrer del Regomir (good for tapas, see ⑪③), to Carrer d'en Gignas or Carrer Ample, and turn left for the **Correu i Telègraf ❾** (Post Office). It is worth popping in to admire the decoration by *Noucentiste* artists Canyellas, Galí, Labarta and Obiols.

Outside is *Cap de Barcelona*, a 64m (210ft) cartoon-like portrait of a woman's head by American Pop artist Roy Lichtenstein. Inspired by Gaudí, the work is made from broken tiles.

La Madre de Déu de la Mercè

Walk down Carrer de la Mercè to the church of **La Madre de Déu de la Mercè ❿** (Plaça de la Mercè; tel: 93 315 27 56; daily 10am–1pm, 6–8pm; free), topped by a statue of the Madonna and child that can be seen from out to sea. La Mercè is the patron saint of Barcelona, and on her saint's day, 24 September, huge models, known as giants, and human pyramids (people standing on each other's shoulders) greet the dignitaries coming out from Mass at the start of the festivities.

Carrer d'Avinyó

From the church, head up **Carrer d'Avinyó**, home to two city landmarks: La Manual Alpargatera, at No. 7, which sells espadrilles; and the Modernista **El Gran Café**, see ⑪④. Halfway down on the right is **Plaça George Orwell ⓫**, named after the author of *Homage to Catalonia*.

Turn left at the top of Carrer d'Avinyó, into the shopping street of Carrer de Ferran, which takes you back to La Rambla.

SANT PERE

An enticing marriage of old and new, this eastern corner of the Old Town, northwest of El Born, is where the rag trade once flourished. Its highlights include the Palau de la Música Catalana and the Mercat de Santa Caterina.

DISTANCE 3km (2 miles)

TIME 3 hours

START Palau de la Música

END Mercat de Santa Caterina

POINTS TO NOTE

This walk is best done in the morning, both to avoid the queues at the Palau de la Música Catalana and to arrive at the Mercat de Santa Caterina in time for lunch. Note that the market closes earlier on Monday *(see p.47 for market hours).*

In the city's Golden Age, the 14th century, Sant Pere was the residential area favoured by the city's wealthy merchants. As the centre of Barcelona's textile trade, it flourished, but mass-production from the late 19th century led to its demise. Visitors have only recently started exploring its historic streets. This tour reveals its highlights.

PALAU DE LA MÚSICA

Start at the **Palau de la Música Catalana ❶** (Carrer de St Francesc de Paula

Above: details of the exterior of the Palau de la Música Catalana.

Did You Know?
Carrer d'Allada-Vermell is what is described in Barcelona as a 'hard' square, created in 1994 by the demolition of a row of housing to bring light into this dense area.

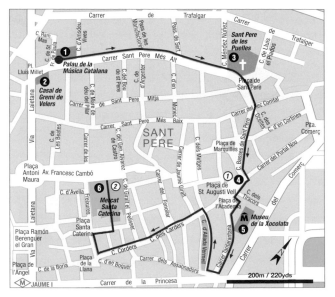

2; tel: 902 442 882; www.palaumusica. org; guided tours daily 10am–3.30pm, Aug until 6pm; booking advisable; charge), built in 1908 by architect Domènech i Montaner and now a World Heritage Site. A Modernista extravaganza, it features lavish decoration of tiles, mosaics and statuary reflecting the Catalan musical tradition.

Oscar Tusquets' recent extension, featuring organic motifs in keeping with the Modernista original, houses a concert hall for chamber music and a restaurant. Tours of the building allow you to admire the stained glass and sculptural decoration of the auditorium.

SANT PERE MÉS ALT

Opposite the Palau, at Carrer Sant Pere Més Alt 1, is the **Casal de Gremi de Velers ②** (Silk Industry Guild), distinguished by fine *esgrafiat* (decorative relief work). Several other textile retailers are based in this street, which was the focus of the medieval trade.

Sant Pere Més Alt terminates at Plaça de Sant Pere and the church of **Sant Pere de les Puelles ③**, a former Benedictine monastery. The street opposite leads to **Plaça de St Augusti Vell ④**, a pleasant little square, and the **Bar Mundial**, see ⑪①.

MUSEU DE LA XOCOLATA

Just beyond, down Carrer d'en Tantarantana, is the **Museu de la Xocolata ⑤** (Carrer del Comerç 36; tel: 93 268 78 78; www. museuxocolata.cat; Mon–Sat 10am–7pm, Sun 10am–3pm; charge). It

charts the history of chocolate (brought to Europe by Hernán Cortés) through photographs and chocolate sculptures, and also runs workshops. The shop, needless to say, is irresistible.

MERCAT DE SANTA CATERINA

Now take **Carrer d'Allada Vermell** opposite and turn left at the top into Carrer dels Carders. Continue to Plaça de la Lana, then right for the **Mercat de Santa Caterina ⑥** (Mon 7.30am–2pm, Tue–Wed, Sat 7.30am–3.30pm, Thur–Fri 7.30am–8.30pm). This stunning three-storey building by the late Enric Miralles (architect of the Scottish Parliament), built on the site of a Dominican monastery, is the centre of urban renewal in the area. Its wonderful roof has coloured tiles above and wood below, in arches like upturned boats. Inside, enjoy a meal at the **Cuines**, see ⑪②. Excavations carried out beneath the market have revealed archaeological remains that are partially open to the public.

Food and Drink

① BAR MUNDIAL
Plaça de St Augusti Vell 1; tel: 93 319 90 56; ; Mon–Sat 1–4pm, 8.30pm–midnight; €€
Opened in 1955 and little changed, this neighbourhood classic does great tapas, with particularly tasty seafood.

② CUINES DE SANTA CATERINA
Avinguda de Francesc Cambó 20; tel: 93 268 99 18; daily 1–4pm, 8–11.30pm; €€
Sit at the bar for a drink and tapas or, for a heartier meal, at one of the tables in this modern, bright emporium within the market. Market-fresh food is used in the Mediterranean, Oriental and vegetarian dishes.

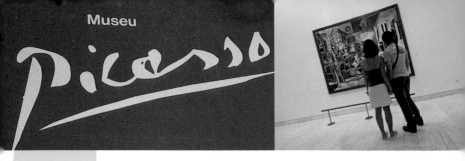

Museu Picasso

LA RIBERA AND EL BORN

The part of the Old Town north of the Via Laietana is La Ribera, a former noble quarter whose name (The Shore) reflects its commercially advantageous waterfront position; within La Ribera is El Born. History mixes with fashion and culture here, with chic boutiques, bars and some of the city's top museums.

DISTANCE 3km (2 miles)
TIME 4 hours
START Jaume I metro
END Estació de França
POINTS TO NOTE

Start early to avoid queues at Museu Picasso (free on first Sun of month).

This walk combines well with the tour of Sant Pere (see p.46) although that is also best done in the morning.

This close-knit residential area owes its character to Jaume I (the Conqueror), under whom Catalonia flourished in its Golden Age of the 14th century. The city's rich were businessmen, not aristocrats, and it was in this waterfront area that merchants brought their wares ashore. They traded in the new stock exchange, prayed in Santa Maria del Mar (the church they swiftly had built in gratitude), jousted on the tilting

Above: the excellent Museu Picasso.

Street Names

Many streets in this area are named after *gremis*, the powerful trade guilds, whose duty was to look after the interests of their members. These include Agullers (needle makers), Argenteria (silversmiths) and Sombreres (hatmakers).

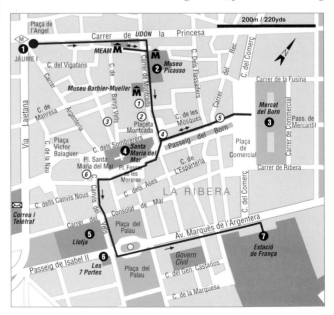

field of El Born and entertained in the sumptuous mansions they erected, notably along Carrer de Montcada.

In later times, a young Pablo Picasso studied at the local art school, where his father also taught; nowadays the Museu Picasso is the area's big crowd-puller.

CARRER MONTCADA

Start at the **Jaume I metro ❶** and stroll down Carrer de la Princesa, which divides the Sant Pere district *(see p.46)* from La Ribera. Opposite **UDON**, Barcelona's first noodle bar, turn right into the slim **Carrer de Montcada**. Named after the fallen in the conquest of Mallorca, it linked the waterfront with the commercial areas during the Golden Age, and the architecturally lavish Catalan-Gothic merchants' mansions that line it reflect its former wealth. Montcada has become museum street supreme, since the authorities started renovating its medieval palaces in 1957.

There are lots of good pit stops near here, such as **Espai Barroc**, see ⑪①, or **El Xampanyet**, see ⑪②.

Museu Picasso

At Carrer de Montcada 15–23 is the **Museu Picasso ❷** (tel: 93 256 30 00; www.museupicasso.bcn.es; Tue–Sun 10am–8pm; charge), spread over five imposing mansions. The entrance is at No. 15, the Palau Aguilar, with a handsome courtyard and first-floor gallery by Marc Safont, architect of the inner patio of the Generalitat. This mansion is connected internally to Palau del Baró de Castellet at No. 17, then by Palau Meca

Casa Mauri and Palau Finestres, the last two used for temporary exhibitions.

There are some 4,000 artworks in the collection, mainly from Picasso's formative years, with sketches in school books and a masterly portrait of his mother, done when he was just 16. Studies for *Las Meninas* from the 1950s are among the few later works. The museum also has an attractive café. Alongside the existing exhibition halls a new building was opened in 2011 to house a Knowledge and Research Centre.

Museu Europeu d'Art Modern

Opposite the Museu Picasso, a short detour west along Barra de Ferro takes you to the **Museu Europeu d'Art Modern** (**MEAM**; Barra de Ferro 5; tel: 93 319 56 93; www.meam.es; Tue–Sun 10am–8pm; charge). Opened in June 2011, this interesting museum offers an original and different vision of contemporary art; its objective is to promote

Above from far left: Museu Picasso sign; admiring the collection; Santa Maria del Mar; Picasso postcards for sale on Carrer de Montcada.

Food and Drink 🍴

① ESPAI BARROC
Carrer de Montcada 20; tel: 93 310 06 73; www.palaudalmases.com; Tue–Sat 8pm–2am, Sun 6–10pm; €€
A cultural highlight in the Palau Dalmases is this Baroque-style bar. There are live recitals on Thursdays.

② EL XAMPANYET
Carrer de Montcada 22; tel: 93 319 70 03; daily noon–4pm, 6.30–11.30pm, closed Aug; €€
Wash down the house speciality, anchovies, with cava, served in wide-brimmed glasses. Tiny bar with a big atmosphere.

Montcada Fresco
A fresco of Jaume I's campaign on the island of Mallorca has been taken from the wall of one of the mansions in Carrer de Montcada and can now be seen in the Palau Nacional *(see p.77).*

Late Starters
The atmosphere
in this area is
transformed at night:
bars that during
the day are hidden
behind closed doors
or lurk in stygian
gloom start to wake
up around 9pm, and
the merry-go-round
of tireless bar-flies
continues until about
4am.

Below: colourful El
Born backstreet.

figurative art from the late 19th century to the present day. Housed in the
stunning 18th-century Palau Gomis,
the varied and compelling collection of
paintings and sculpture covers three
floors and is accessed through a wide
courtyard lined with sculptures.

Other Montcada Galleries
Back on Carrer de Montcada at No. 14
is the **Museu Barbier-Mueller** (tel: 93
310 45 16; www.barbier-mueller.ch;
Tue–Fri 11am–7pm, Sat–Sun 11am–
8pm; charge). What the collection of
Pre-Columbian art lacks in size, it
more than compensates for in terms
of prestige, with superb Aztec, Mayan
and Inca jewellery and artefacts.

Continue along the street for another
contemporary art gallery that usually has
notable exhibitions: **Galeria Maeght**,
housed in the Palau Cervelló at No. 25,
is part of the French Maeght gallery
group, which owes its success to the

early support in Cannes of Provence-
based artists Matisse, Bonnard, Van
Dongen and Miró.

EL BORN

Carrer de Montcada ends at Plaçeta
de Montcada, where it hits the **Passeig del Born**. Nearby, on Carrer de
Banys Vells, parallel to Montcada, is
the excellent historic wine bar **Va de
Vi**, see ⑪③. The main strip here is a
fashionistas' haunt, home to chic bars
and cafés, see ⑪④ and ⑪⑤, and
numerous designer boutiques.

Mercat del Born
A detour east along Passeig del Born
takes you past Carrer dels Flassaders,
where there are more boutiques and, at
the end of the Passseig, Josep Fontserè
i Mestre's 19th-century wrought-iron
Mercat del Born ❸, until 1971, a
wholesale food market. The structure
is being remodelled as a cultural centre,
but work has been delayed due to the
discovery of pre-18th-century houses
on the site. A viewing platform can
be accessed on Carrer de la Fusina, on
the market's northern edge.

SANTA MARIA DEL MAR

At the western end of Passeig del Born
is **Santa Maria del Mar ❹** (tel: 93 310
23 90; Mon–Sat 9am–1.30pm, 4.30–
8pm, Sun 10.30am–1.30pm, 4.30–8pm;
free), built from 1329–84 by the maritime enterprises that brought wealth
to this part of town. It is a fine example
of the Catalan-Gothic style, with hori-

zontal lines, flat terraced roofing, open spaces and octagonal towers. Stand by the main door to appreciate the sense of space and the warm light that enters through the rose window. The striking blue window in the second chapel on the left in the ambulatory commemorates the 1992 Olympic Games.

Surrounding Squares

In **Plaça Fossar de les Moreres**, the square beside the church, note the iron monument topped by a flame; this commemorates the martyrs of the Bourbon succession in 1714. Beyond it, **Plaça de Santa Maria del Mar** is a buzzy square with appealing cafés and bars, such as **La Vinya del Senyor**, see ⑥. Just to the right is **Carrer de l'Argenteria**, one of the busiest restaurant streets in town, where there are regular queues in the evening, as people wait to get into the popular tapas bars and restaurants.

THE LLOTJA

On the opposite (port) side of the square, turn down Carrer dels Canvis Vells, which leads to the Carrer del Consolat de Mar and the **Llotja** ❺ (closed to visitors), the former stock exchange – a handsome 14th-century building with a magnificent Gothic hall.

Picasso's father taught at the Escola de Belles Arts (School of Fine Arts) that occupied the upper part of the building. The **Reial Academia Catalana de Belles Arts de Sant Jordi** (tours by appointment Mon–Fri 10am–2pm, email: museu@racba.org) still occupies

part of the building. Its small museum has drawings by the 19th-century Romantic painter Mariano Fortuny.

7 Portes

Across the busy Passeig de Isabel II, in an arcaded 19th-century building, is Barcelona's most famous restaurant, **7 Portes** ❻ *(see p.119)*. Peek through the windows to see the handsome panelled interior and imagine Picasso, Lorca and the rest of the artistic crowd enjoying a dish of its speciality black rice or paella.

Further along the road is the grand **Estació de França** ❼ *(see picture, right)*, the city's original international train terminus, now restored, and well worth a look in for its handsome iron-and-glass 19th-century structure.

Church Concerts
Concerts are held in the church of Santa Maria del Mar – check the church noticeboard for details. Sit on the steps in the side chapels near the front to avoid the six second acoustic delay.

Food and Drink 🍴

③ VA DE VI
Carrer de Banys Vells 16; tel: 93 319 29 00; Tue–Wed 6pm–1am, Thur 6pm–2am, Fri–Sat 6pm–3am; €–€€
Cavernous old wine bar with a modern designer touch. Great place to try the best of Spain's wines and local artisanal produce.

④ EUSKAL ETXEA TABERNA
Plaçeta de Montcada 1–3; tel: 93 176 89 84; restaurant: Mon–Sat 1–4pm, 8pm–midnight; bar: Mon–Fri 10am–midnight, Sat–Sun 10–1am; €€€
Superb Basque tapas bar and restaurant.

⑤ SANDWICH & FRIENDS
Passeig del Born, 27; tel: 93 310 07 86; Sun–Thur 9–1am, Fri–Sat 9–2am; €
Trendy café dominated by a huge mural. A tremendous variety of sandwiches filled with all sorts of unusual combinations.

⑥ LA VINYA DEL SENYOR
Plaça de Santa Maria 5; tel: 93 310 33 79; Tue–Thur and Sun noon–1am, Fri–Sat noon–2am; €€€€
The Lord's Vineyard is a classic wine bar in a great spot on the square. Excellent tapas and an incredibly wide selection of wines.

EL RAVAL

The city's old working-class district still has a slightly raw edge that is reminiscent of a seedy past, but urban redevelopment has laid out new spaces and a fabulous contemporary art museum, the MACBA.

Lively Nightlife

El Raval comes to life at night, with a variety of bars and clubs, such as Rita Blue in Plaça de Sant Augustí or Bar Almirall, which dates from 1860, on Carrer de Joaquín Costa. The latter is good for a drink after visiting the nearby MACBA.

DISTANCE 2.5km (1½ miles)

TIME 2 hours

START La Rambla (top end)

END Palau Güell

POINTS TO NOTE

This walk runs parallel to La Rambla, on its southwestern side. It is best to do it during the daytime, but not on Tuesday, when MACBA (the Contemporary Art Museum) is closed.

On the opposite side of La Rambla to the Barri Gòtic is the working-class area of the city that was incorporated into the Old Town with the building of the medieval city walls. El Raval (literally, 'The Slum') stretches from La Rambla to the Ronda de Sant Pau and the Avinguda del Paral.lel. The district of old high-rise tenements was once one of the world's most densely populated, with many immigrants from poorer regions of Spain housed here.

The area towards the waterfront was a haunt of sailors, delinquents and addicts. In the 1920s it was dubbed the

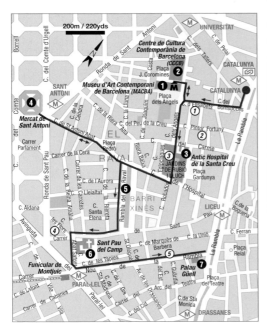

Food and Drink 🍴

① DOS PALILLOS

Carrer d'Elisabets 9; 93 304 05 13; www.dospalillos.com; Thur–Sat 1.30–3.30pm, 7.30–11.30pm, Tue–Wed 7.30–11.30pm; €€
This is a smart, trendy place with the unusual concept of a choice of Asian food or Spanish tapas, presented and cooked to a high standard. Note that lunch is only served from Thursday to Saturday.

② BIOCENTER

Carrer del Pintor Fortuny 25; tel: 93 301 45 83; www.restaurantebio center.es; daily 1–5pm, 8–11.15pm; €
This well-established, friendly vegetarian restaurant does healthy, hearty four-course set-price menus.

Barri Xinès (*Barrio Chino* in Spanish), meaning Chinese quarter, though the Chinese were never in evidence here.

Regeneration Area

The area has been undergoing a metamorphosis, thanks to municipal funding. Trendy bars, shops and art galleries now sit side by side with more seedy spots: do not be surprised to see sex workers on street corners in broad daylight. Regeneration has been in progress since the late 1990s, with whole blocks of tenements torn down to open up the area. There is still a large immigrant population here (over 47 percent are from outside Spain), making it one of the most ethnically diverse parts of Europe.

MACBA

From the top of La Rambla, take the second right down Carrer del Bonsucces and Carrer d'Elisabets. Like all the streets in this area, it retains many good traditional bars and some quirky new restaurants, including the new-style **Dos Palillos**, see ⑪① and, on the parallel street, Carrer Pintor Fortuny, the **Biocenter**, see ⑪②.

Follow signs to Plaça dels Àngels and Richard Meier's ice-white Modernist-style **Museu d'Art Contemporani de Barcelona ❶** (MACBA; tel: 93 412 08 10; www.macba.es; June–Sept Mon and Wed–Sat 11am–8pm, Oct–May Mon and Wed–Fri 11am–7.30pm, Sat 10am–8pm, Sun 10am–3pm all year; charge), with the neighbouring Convent dels Àngels acting as an outpost. The front slopes are popular with skate-boarders. On Thursdays in summer (July–Sept) MACBA remains open until midnight, at a reduced price of €3. Concerts are often held in the bar on these late nights.

The Collection

Arranged over three floors, the gallery showcases post-war Catalan, Spanish and international art from *c*.1950, with works by artists including Antonio Saura, Tàpies, Joseph Beuys, Jeff Wall and Susana Solano. The permanent collection is displayed on a rotating basis, but the main attractions are the cutting-edge temporary exhibitions by contemporary artists. La Central del MACBA is the museum's bookshop and reference centre. **Capella MACBA** is the convent's 15th-century Gothic church with the only Renaissance chapel in Barcelona.

CENTRE DE CULTURA CONTEMPORÀNIA

This melding of ancient and modern, at which the Barcelonans are so good, can be seen again at the Plaça de Joan Coromines, which links the MACBA with the old Casa de Caritat, formerly a poorhouse and orphanage that has become the magnificent, four-storey **Centre de Cultura Contemporània de Barcelona ❷** (CCCB; Carrer de Montalegre 5; tel: 93 306 41 00; www. cccb.org; Tue–Sun 11am–8pm, exhibition times can vary; charge). The centre, which is entered via a ramp in the basement, puts on exhibitions,

Theatre Street
Avinguda del Paral.lel, on the south side of El Raval, was once renowned as Europe's 'Street of Theatres'. Famous for vaudeville, music halls and cabaret, its most famous venue was El Molino (The Windmill), called the Petit Moulin Rouge after its Parisian counterpart, though it changed its name when 'red' became an unwise word to use during the Franco era. Opened in 1899, it did not quite manage to see out the 20th century. Other larger theatres remain, most staging musicals or farces that attract coach parties from out of town.
The street name, Paral.lel, supplanted the existing Calle Marqués de Duero in 1794, when a Frenchman, Pierre François André Méchain, discovered that the avenue lay exactly along the parallel latitude 44° 44' North.

concerts, dance and films. There is also a bar-restaurant and a bookshop.

Also on Plaça de Joan Coromines is a new university faculty building and the **Centre d'Estudis i Recursos Culturas** (CERC; tel: 93 402 25 65; www.diba.es/cerc; free). Step inside to see the lovely, tiled 18th-century courtyard, **Pati Manning**, with an Art Deco St George.

At the back of the courtyard is a last vestige of religiosity in the area, the church of **Santa Maria de Monte-alegre**, where Mass is still held.

Above: Sant Pau del Camp.

Slaughtered
West of El Raval, the former slaughter house is marked by Joan Miró's tile totem, *Dona i Ocell* (Woman and Bird, *see picture on p.28, bottom left*).

ANTIC HOSPITAL DE LA SANTA CREU

Walk back down Carrer dels Àngels to the 15th-century **Antic Hospital de la Santa Creu ❸** (Carrer del Carme/Carrer de l'Hospital; no tel; Mon–Fri 9am–8pm, Sat 9am–2pm; free), a con-valescent house set up in the 15th-century and the city's principal hospital until 1910, when Santa Creu i Sant Paul was built near the Sagrada Família *(see p.72)*. Some of the building houses the headquarters of the Royal Academy of Medicine, but the rest is devoted to the Massana Art School, the Institute of Catalan Studies and the Library of Catalonia.

On the right as you enter is the Casa de Convalescència (Convalescence House), its gardens richly decorated with 17th-century Baroque tiles by Llorens Passolles. Hidden in the gardens is **El Jardin**, a perfect stop for lunch on the terrace, see ③.

Exit through the main entrance in Carrer de l'Hospital. Just outside is **La Capella** (Tue–Sat noon–2pm, 4–8pm, Sun 11am–2pm; free), the hospital's 15th-century chapel, now an exhibition space for contemporary art.

Carrer de l'Hospital
On **Carrer de l'Hospital** are herbal-ists, pharmacists and Arab pastry stores, reflecting the quirky mix of tra-ditional and ethnic in this area. One of its side streets, the pedestrian Carrer de la Riera Baixa, is lined with vin-tage and second-hand clothes shops.

Continuing along Carrer de l'Hos-pital, head west on to Carrer de Sant Antoni Abat, which extends to **Mercat de Sant Antoni ❹**, a large, attractive 19th-century market hall. During the week this serves as a food market, with clothes and haberdashers' stalls behind the encircling blinds, and on Sunday, from 9am–2pm, it is given over to a

---

Food and Drink 🍴

③ EL JARDIN
Carrer de l'Hospital 56; tel: 93 329 15 50; www.eljardinbarcelona.es; Mar–Oct daily 10am–11pm, Nov–Feb Mon–Sat 10am–10pm; €
In the lovely gardens of the old hospital, this tapas bar is ideal for a freshly produced snack and a drink in the sun or shade.

④ CA L'ISIDRE
Carrer de les Flors 12; tel: 93 441 11 39; www.calisidre.com; Mon–Sat 1.30–4pm, 8.30–11pm; €€€ (set lunch Mon–Fri €€)
A family-owned restaurant producing fine traditional cuisine with a contemporary twist, and sumptuous desserts. Excellent service.

⑤ LONDON BAR
Nou de la Rambla 34; tel: 93 318 52 61; Mon–Thur 10am–3am, Fri 10am–3.30am, Sat 6pm–3.30am; €
Apart from the addition of a big television screen, this historic pub (established 1910) has changed little since Miró and Picasso drank here. Drinks only, no food.

lively market for second-hand books, coins and videos. The building is undergoing major restoration, during which the food market has moved to a site close by on the Ronda Sant Antoni. The Sunday book market has been moved just to the north of the main market building. Restoration work is being carried out in phases and there is no definite reopening date as yet.

Rambla del Raval

Walking back along Carrer de Sant Antoni Abat into Carrer de l'Hospital will bring you to the top of the **Rambla del Raval** ❺. This tree-lined thoroughfare was only relatively recently created by bulldozing more than five blocks through the heart of the *Barri Xinès*, but it has already brought wealth to the area in the shape of bars, galleries and cafés.

SANT PAU DEL CAMP

At the bottom of the Rambla turn right into Carrer de Sant Pau to **Sant Pau del Camp** ❻ (tel: 93 441 00 01; Mon–Sat 10am–1.30pm, 4–7pm, times may vary; charge), Barcelona's oldest church, dating from Roman times. A door to the right leads to a pretty little cloister with trefoil and cinquefoil arches. A gravestone bears an inscription to Guifre II Borrell, who in 897 became the second ruler of the Barcelona dynasty.

At the crossroads turn left down Carrer de l'Abat Safont or, if you would like a smart lunch, take Carrer de les Flors diagonally opposite for **Ca L'Isidre** at No. 12, see ⑪④.

PALAU GÜELL

Finally, walk down Carrer Nou de la Rambla, past the **London Bar**, see ⑪⑤, to the **Palau Güell** ❼ (Carrer Nou de la Rambla 3; tel: 93 472 57 75; www.palauguell.cat; Apr–Sept Tue–Sun 10am–8pm, Oct–Mar 10am–5.30pm; charge), designed by Gaudí from 1885–9 as a town house for his patron, Count Eusebi Güell and now reopened after extensive renovation.

With this building, the architect embarked on a period of fertile creativity, alternating elements of the Gothic with Arabic design. The house is structured around an enormous salon, from which a conical roof covered in pieces of tiling emerges to preside over an unusual landscape of capriciously placed battlements, balustrades and strangely shaped chimneys.

Above from far left: El Raval bookshop; one of the many El Raval bars.

Did You Know? Although Eusebi Güell lived in the Palau Güell for two years, he apparently never visited the extraordinary roof, decorated with multi-coloured chimneys in Gaudí's characteristic broken-tile mosaic, known as *trencadis*.

Below: Juicy Jones juice bar, Carrer de l'Hospital.

THE WATERFRONT

Rejuvenated for the Barcelona Olympic Games in 1992, the waterfront area added an exciting new dimension to the city. This tour takes you through Port Vell (Old Port) and the regenerated area of Barceloneta.

DISTANCE 4km (2¼ miles)
TIME 3 hours
START Museu Marítim
END Torre de Jaume I
POINTS TO NOTE

This is a gentle-paced walk that can be done at any time of day or in the evening, although note that the Museu d'Història de Catalunya closes on Monday.

Shipping Links
Barcelona has direct links by ship with the ports in Genoa, Rome, Algiers-Oran, Ibiza, Mallorca and Menorca.

Commercial maritime activity moved out of Barcelona's original port in the 1990s, leaving Port Vell, the Old Port, with few concerns other than round-the-clock leisure. A focus of the city, this is where people come to spend idle hours, watching vessels from the yacht clubs pass beneath the swing bridge on the pedestrian Rambla de Mar, seeing who is sipping champagne on the huge posh yachts in the marina, or admiring the visiting tall ships.

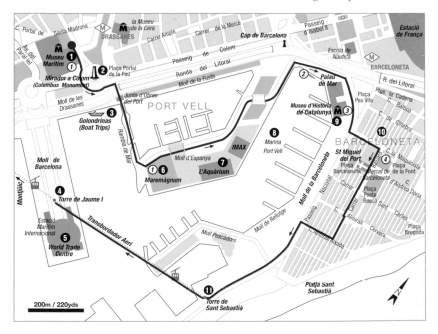

On the northeast (or far) side of the port is Barceloneta, the old fishermen's quarter *(see p.59)*, while on the south side is the cruise-line terminal.

OLD SHIPYARDS

Beyond the bottom of La Rambla are the Drassanes, the city's formidable former shipyards, now home to the Museu Marítim, a good place to begin a tour of waterfront Barcelona.

Proud History

Erected in 1378, enclosed by the city's 15th-century outer wall (which stretches round into Avinguda del Paral.lel, where the Portal de Santa Madrona tower and gateway remain) and greatly enlarged in the 17th century, the huge, shed-like Drassanes launched thousands of ships. At their height they were turning out 30 war galleys at a time, as when the Christian West prepared for a final showdown with the Muslim Ottomans in 1571 at Lepanto off the Greek coast.

Museu Marítim

The **Museu Marítim ❶** (Avinguda de les Drassanes; tel: 93 342 99 20; www. museumaritimbarcelona.com; daily 10am–8pm; charge) charts Catalonia's seafaring history with a fine collection of fishing boats and model ships, including a full-scale replica of Don Juan of Austria's victorious flagship, the *Reial* (the original of which was built here). The museum has been undergoing a comprehensive remodelling since 2009 and the permanent exhibits

are not on view at the time of writing. Temporary displays are still open to the public and the new, more interactive museum is due to open in 2013.

Plaça Portal de la Pau

The nearby Mirador a Colom *(see p.35)*, stands in the **Plaça Portal de la Pau ❷** (Gate of Peace Square). It was through a gate on this site that Christopher Columbus triumphantly entered the city on his return from the West Indies in April 1493.

PORT VELL

Moll de les Drassanes

In front of the statue is the **Moll de les Drassanes** (*moll* means wharf), from where **Las Golondrinas ❸** (Swallows) pleasure boats (tel: 93 442 31 06; www.lasgolondrinas.com; summer daily 11.45am–7.30pm, rest of year: slightly shorter hours; charge) run trips to the entrance of the commercial harbour or to the Olympic port.

To the left is the **Junta d'Obres del Port**, the Port Authority building constructed in 1907 as a reception point.

Above from far left: sunbathing on the boardwalk; café tables by the port; cycling along the waterfront.

Below: the Mirador a Colom; yacht in the harbour; one of the Golondrinas.

Food and Drink 🍽

① TAPA TAPA
Maremàgnum Centre; floor 0, local 10; tel: 93 225 86 97; daily 11am–1am; €€€
There are plenty of dishes to choose from at this traditional tapas restaurant with a modern touch. The bright space has a marine theme and one of the most privileged terraces in the city – views over the harbour are spectacular.

Did You Know?
The Golondrinas have been plying these waters since the 1888 Universal Exhibition. Be sure to choose one of the older and more elegant boats, which have names such as *Lolita* and *Encarnación*.

Above: Rambla de Mar footbridge; ship's rigging.

Moll de Barcelona

Today, cruise-line passengers embark at the Moll Adossat further south, but high-speed boats to the Balearics disembark at the Estació Marítim on the 500m (1,640ft) **Moll de Barcelona**, which runs at right angles to the Moll de les Drassanes.

The jetty also has the 119m (390ft) **Torre de Jaume I ❹** link for the cross-harbour cable car, the **Transbordador Aeri**, erected in 1931 and leading from Montjuïc; it continues to the Torre de Sant Sebastià *(see p.59)*, at the south-eastern end of the port.

At the end of the Moll de Barcelona is the **World Trade Centre ❺**, designed by architect I.M. Pei (of Paris's Louvre pyramid fame) and housing a commercial centre with offices, restaurants and a five-star hotel.

Moll d'Espanya

Walk over the undulating wooden Rambla de Mar footbridge to the **Moll d'Espanya**, Port Vell's main jetty. This is a popular place for families and young Barcelonans at weekends and evenings, with the **Maremàgnum ❻** shopping mall, Imax cinema and **L'Aquàrium ❼** (tel: 93 221 74 74; www.aquariumbcn. com; July–Aug daily 9.30am–11pm, June and Sept 9.30am–9.30pm, Oct–May Mon–Fri 9.30am–9pm, Sat–Sun until 9.30pm; charge). In the aquarium, the blue-shimmering tanks show what swims in the surrounding seas, and a glass tunnel leads visitors among sharks and rays.

The **Maremàgnum** is home to several good refreshment options but **Tapa Tapa** provides great views while you eat, see ⑪① *(p.57)*.

Outside the Imax cinema is a replica of Narcís Monturiol's wooden submarine, *Ictineu II,* that entered the waters here in 1864 *(see box, right)*.

Moll de la Fusta and the Marina

The **Moll d'Espanya** leads ashore to the old timber wharf, the **Moll de la Fusta** (Wood Wharf), redesigned as a palm-lined promenade in the late 1980s by Manuel de Solà-Morales.

W Barcelona

Rising 26 floors above the Mediterranean, and marking the entrance to Barcelona's harbour, is an avant-garde icon of the city's dynamic post-modern architecture. Shaped like a billowing sail, the long awaited W Barcelona hotel, the work of Spanish architect Ricardo Bofill, opened in 2009.

Where these two *molls* meet you will see the **Marina Port Vell** ❽ always bustling with yachts on the move, and here you can climb aboard the **Luz de Gas Port Vell** floating bar, see ⑪②. Adjacent, in the Porta del Pau, is American Pop artist Roy Lichtenstein's colourful *Cap de Barcelona* (Barcelona Head; *see p.45*).

Museu d'Història de Catalunya
This was once a dock area that bustled with industry, but the only warehouse remaining is Elies Rogent's 1878 brick-built Magatzem General, now the Palau de Mar. Part of the building is used to house the excellent **Museu d'Història de Catalunya** ❾ (Plaça de Pau Vila 3; tel: 93 225 47 00; www.mhcat.net; Tue, Thur–Sat 10am–7pm, Wed 10am–8pm, Sun 10am–2.30pm; charge). It covers two substantial floors: the first takes the story up to the 18th century; the second begins with industrialisation and includes memories of the Franco years. The museum's rooftop restaurant has a great view over the harbour, see ⑪③.

BARCELONETA

At the end of the Marina quay is **Barceloneta** ❿, once home to the city's fishing community, and created in 1753 to house citizens who had been usurped by the building of the Ciutadella fortress *(see p.61)*. The architect, military engineer Juan Martin de Cermeño, designed two-storey terraces on a grid system to allow volleys from the castle to be directed down the streets.

Though this is still a close-knit community, its small bars and restaurants have become popular with people from across the city. Its proximity to the beach is also a draw, and increasingly flats are being let out to tourists.

In the heart of the district is a market, remodelled in 2007 by Josep Mias incorporating material from the area's 19th-century market. The market bar, **El Paco**, see ⑪④, is a good place to stop for snacks. Note also the Moll del Rellotge (Clock Wharf), named after the clock tower (closed to the public) that once served as a lighthouse.

Cable Car Ride
An option now is to continue walking for around 15 minutes to the end of the harbour and the **Torre de Sant Sebastià** ⑪. A lift ascends the iron hulk to a platform from which the cable cars fly over the harbour back to the Torre de Jaume I. Just beyond, towering above the boardwalk, is the W Barcelona hotel *(see margin, p.58)*.

Above from far left: the boardwalk by Maremàgnum; a Golondrina in Port Vell; night-time illuminations; cable car over the port.

Helicopter Ride
Cat Helicòpters (tel: 93 224 07 10; www.cathelicopters.com) offers 10-minute flights over the city, covering the Olympic sites, Barça football stadium, Tibidabo, Park Güell, the Sagrada Família, the Fòrum and port. The heliport is located at Moll Adossat, the cruise-ship quay.

An Idealist Inventor

Taking pride of place in the old port is a replica of *Ictineu II*, the world's first combustion-powered submarine. Its inventor was Narcís Monturiol (1819–85), who came up with the design after witnessing the dangerous work of coral divers in Cadaqués, north of Barcelona. An idealist with socialist beliefs, Monturiol was briefly exiled to France where he met the Icarians, like-minded intellectuals who went on to try to establish Icaria, a Utopian colony in America. It failed, but the name lived on in Barcelona's industrial district, Nova Icària; this became the site of the Olympic Village, where it was hoped that Utopian values might prevail.

8 CIUTADELLA

Parc de la Ciutadella is the city's favourite open space, with gardens, boating lake, museums and zoo, making a pleasant escape from the city clamour. To the north you will find the inspiring Museu de la Música and Els Encants, the bustling flea market located in the developing Plaça de les Glòries.

DISTANCE 5km (3 miles)
TIME 4 hours
START Arc de Triomf
END Plaça de les Glòries Catalanes
POINTS TO NOTE
This route starts at the Arc de Triomf metro but could begin anywhere in the park. Its second leg could be taken by tram, or as a separate trip.

Next to the Old Town's La Ribera quarter, inland from Barceloneta, lies Parc de la Ciutadella, a large and felic-itous green space. An unhurried stroll through the park may be enough of an outing for a visitor, but if you feel energetic it could also be combined with a trip to the Teatre Nacional de Catalunya and the excellent Museu de la Música, as well as to the sprawling flea market of Els Encants at Plaça de les Glòries Catalanes.

Above: the Catalan parliament building, located within the park; flamingos at the zoo; traffic lights by the Torre Agbar.

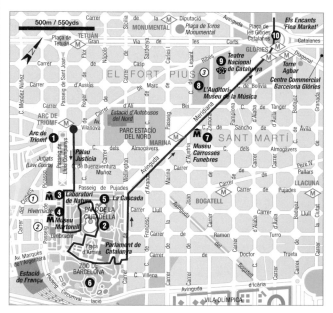

ARC DE TRIOMF

On the north side of the park is the **Arc de Triomf ❶**, by the metro station of the same name. This bulky brick monument, echoing its namesake on the Champs–Élysées in Paris, was designed by Josep Vilaseca i Casanovas as the entrance to the Universal Exhibition of 1888, which was staged in the park.

Walk down the Passeig de Lluís Companys, ever-popular with men playing *petanca* (boules). The law courts are on the left, and, if you look back up the avenue, the Collserola hills provide a grand backdrop. If you want to eat before continuing into the park proper, turn into Carrer del Comerç, on your right, for **Santa Maria**, see ⑪①. Alternatively, for a meal or takeaway carry on down the west side of the park on Passeig de Picasso and try the Japanese **Ikibana** at No. 32, see ⑪② *(p.63)*.

PARC DE LA CIUTADELLA

At the bottom of Passeig de Lluís Companys is the main entrance to the 30-hectare (75-acre) **Parc de la Ciutadella ❷** (daily 10am–sunset; free). It is easy to while away time here, in the shade of deciduous, coniferous and palm trees, all well labelled, and now inhabited by squawking parakeets escaped from cages on La Rambla.

The park takes its name from a star-shaped citadel built by Felipe V to control the city after his successful siege in 1714 *(see p.26)*. The fortress was later torn down and the park given to the city

to turn into a public space by General Prim, when he became Spain's president in 1869 (he was assassinated only a year later). It was laid out by Josep Fontserré (for whom a young Antoni Gaudí worked briefly) in 1873.

Castell dels Tres Dragons

Most of the buildings designed for the 1888 Universal Exhibition were hastily erected and not intended to last. An exception is Modernista architect Lluís Domènech i Montaner's Café-Restaurant, to the right of the park as you enter, and more often known as the **Castell dels Tres Dragons** (Castle of the Three Dragons).

This crenellated red-brick fort, modelled on the Llotja (Stock Exchange) in Valencia and impossible to miss, never opened as a restaurant but instead served as an arts-and-crafts centre and the architect's studio for a period after the exhibition closed.

A parliament assembled here in 1917, and in 1934 it opened its doors to the Museu de Zoologia, now the **Laboratori de Natura ❸** (tel: 93 256 22 22; www.museuciencies.bcn.cat; closed for renovation, check for details

Above from far left: the park's monumental Cascada fountain; playground fun; sea lions at the zoo; interior of the Umbracle palm house.

Liberal General General Prim, who wanted a model monarchy in Spain, once stated, 'Looking for a democratic monarch in Europe is like trying to find an atheist in heaven.'

Food and Drink 🍴

① SANTA MARIA
Carrer del Comerç 17; tel: 93 315 12 27; www.santarestaurant.word press.com; Tue–Thur noon–11pm, Fri–Sat noon–midnight; €€
Chef Paco Guzman promotes the rare idea of gourmet food at manageable prices, with his dainty little dishes of Mediterranean and Oriental extraction.

Above: exterior of the Umbracle; fountain statue.

Passeig de Picasso

This avenue, which runs along the western edge of the park, was designed by Josep Fontserré as part of the Ciutadella redevelopment. Look out, on the part of the road near the Umbracle, for Antoni Tàpies' 1981 sculpture *Homenatje a Picasso* (Homage to Picasso), enclosed within a glass box. Some good bars and bicycle-hire shops can be found here.

before you visit). It will house a new research centre, plus the zoological and geological collections. A new natural history and science museum, the Museu Blau, opened in 2011 in the Fòrum *(see p.67)*.

Museu Martorell

Further on is the neoclassical **Museu Martorell** ❹ (tel: 93 256 22 22; www.museuciencies.bcn.cat; closed for renovation, check for details before you visit), which was home to the city's first public museum, the former Museu de Geologia. The new museum will feature a permanent exhibition called 'A not-so-natural history: public and natural history from cabinets to museums'.

Greenhouses, Cascada and Lake

To either side of the Museu de Geologia lie the greenhouses of the **Hivernacle**, and the **Umbracle** palm house.

From here, cross back over the main path to **La Cascada** ❺, a monumental fountain with Neptune, nymphs and grottoes by Fontserré. Take a break in front of the fountain at the Cascada Qiosc, which sells drinks and snacks. A few steps further on is a boating lake (€6 for 30 minutes for two people), where life slows to a ripple, and ducks bask on the banks for your admiration.

Plaça d'Armes

Beyond the lake is the **Plaça d'Armes**, where *El Desconsol* (The Inconsolable), a Josep Llimona damsel, crouches in the central pond. The buildings each side of the square are all that remain of the citadel built by the victorious Bourbon

king, Felipe V. Later used as a prison, the buildings were captured by Napoleon, demolished, rebuilt, handed back to the town, then bombed in the Civil War. On the west side is a chapel and, beside it, the former local governor's palace (1748), which is now a school.

On the opposite, eastern, side of the square is the former **arsenal**, which was made into a royal palace, when the park became a leisure ground in the late 19th century. This is where the **Parlament de Catalunya** sits today, guarded by the Mossos d'Esquadra, the Catalan police.

Parc Zoològic

The main avenue in the park ends at **Plaça del General Prim**, dominated by an equestrian statue of the general. This is also the entrance to the **Zoo de Barcelona** ❻ (tel: 93 225 67 80; www. zoobarcelona.cat; daily Apr–Sept 10am–7pm, Mar and Oct 10am–6pm, Nov–Feb 10am–5pm; charge). Its Aquarama dolphin show (hourly at weekends) is the big attraction, although there are also sea lions, elephants, hippos, monkeys and farmyard animals.

NORTH OF THE PARK

Exit the zoo on to **Carrer de Wellington**, where you can catch a tram up Avinguda Meridiana, past the **Museu Carrosses Funebres** ❼ (Carrer de Sancho de Avila 2; tel: 93 484 17 10; Mon–Fri 10am–1pm, 4–6pm, Sat–Sun 10am–1pm; free), near the Marina metro station. One of the city's more curious museums, it displays hearses from the 18th century to the 1950s.

L'Auditori

Alight at the same metro stop for Rafael Moneo's 1999 **L'Auditori 8** (Carrer de Lepant 150; tel: 93 247 93 00; www.auditori.com; information desk daily 8am–10pm, box office Mon–Sat 3–9pm and Sun 1 hour prior to performances; closed Aug), home to the city's resident orchestra, the Orquestra Simfònica de Barcelona (OBC), with a 2,500-seat symphonic hall and a smaller, more intimate space for chamber music. There is also a decent café, see ⑨③.

The Auditori is home to the excellent **Museu de la Música** (tel: 93 256 36 50; www.bcn.es/museumusica; Mon, Wed–Sat 10am–9pm, Sun 10am–8pm; charge). It has instruments from all over the world, with an audioguide so that you can hear what they sound like, and it also gives a comprehensive account of how Western music developed.

Teatre Nacional de Catalunya

Beside the Auditori is the vast neo-classical National Theatre, the **Teatre Nacional de Catalunya 9** (TNC; information tel: 93 306 57 00; box office tel: 902 10 12 12; www.tnc.cat), designed by Ricardo Bofill and opened in 1998. Plays are generally performed in Catalan, so dance productions may be more accessible to visitors.

Gloriès Flea Market

At the top of Avinguda Meridiana is the **Plaça de les Glòries Catalanes** *(see margin, right)* **10**, an elaborate traffic junction that the architect of the Eix-ample *(see p.68)* originally hoped

would become the new city centre. There is even a park in the middle of the junction .

One exit leads to **Els Encants** (Mon, Wed, Fri, Sat 9am–5pm; furniture auctions Mon, Wed, Fri 7.15–9am), a huge flea market, though not really a place for genuine bargains. (Better shopping opportunities may be available at the nearby **Centre Commercial Barcelona Glòries**.) Proposals to move the market are yet to be decided.

Torre Agbar

Towering over the area is the lipstick-shaped **Torre Agbar**, designed by the French architect Jean Nouvel, named after the water company **Ag**uas de **Bar**celona and opened in 2005. Known locally as the Suppository, the 144m (472ft) building is Barcelona's third tallest, and features a glass facade that glows in shifting hues of red and blue at night, thanks to 4,500 LED lights – inspired, according to Nouvel, by Gaudí.

Above from far left: Aquarama dolphin show; taking a break in the park; L'Auditori; Torre Agbar.

Les Glòries

A huge urban development centred on this square is well under way bringing new arts, education and health facilities to the city as well as easing traffic problems. The DHUB arts organisation has commissioned state-of-the-art premises to be built here, which will house museums that are currently in Palau Reial de Pedralbes *(see p.83)*. Already under construction, it is expected to open during 2013.

Food and Drink

② IKIBANA

Passeig de Picasso 32; tel: 93 295 67 32; www.ikibanagastro club.com; daily 1.30–4pm, 8pm–12.30am; €€
East meets West at this Japanese-Brazilian fusion restaurant. Some delectable sashimi, sushi and tempura, plus Kobe burgers and Brazilian desserts. There's a good value set lunch and take-away available.

③ BAR LANTERNA

L'Auditori, Avinguda Meridiana; tel: 93 247 93 00; Mon–Fri 9am–7pm, also on concert days until one hour after end of concert; €
There aren't many obvious places to eat and drink around the Auditori and Teatre Nacional, but the Auditori does have this bar-café serving sandwiches and snacks.

ALONG THE BEACH

Imported golden sand, which is cleaned daily, extends up the coast from Barceloneta, past the Port Olímpic to Poble Nou, Diagonal Mar and the Parc de Fòrum. It is ideal for a lengthy stroll.

Wintery Walks
Don't automatically discount this route if you visit outside the peak summer months, as the waterfront is a great place for a stroll year-round. In fact, there is something especially satisfying about tucking into a warming alfresco paella lunch after, or part way through, a bracing winter walk.

DISTANCE 7km (4 miles)
TIME 3 hours
START Platja de Sant Sebastià
END Fòrum
POINTS TO NOTE
In summer, this walk is best done in the morning or late afternoon, when the sun is not too strong. Sant Sebastià, the beach closest to the centre of the Old Town, catches the last of the day's sun, so an option is to do the walk in the opposite direction, ending in Barceloneta.

The curving waterfront strip covered on this route is one of the major legacies of the 1992 Barcelona Olympics. Prior to the regeneration, this was an industrial area, characterised by smoking factories and shunting yards, and in steady decline; only the foolhardy ventured onto the beach for a dip in the sea.

The whole area was planned as a smart new residential quarter, with 2,000 apartments in six-storey blocks covering 63 hectares (155 acres), and initially used as the Vila Olímpica to accommodate the competing athletes.

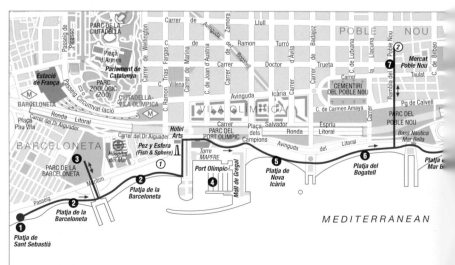

THE BEACHES

There are eight sections of beach along this coast, all well served with showers, bars, Creu Roja (Red Cross) emergency posts and imaginative seats from which you can catch the sun and contemplate the Mediterranean. The main railway line along the coast, serving Estació de França, is buried beneath the Ronda Litoral, which divides the beach from the buildings behind, giving the whole seafront an open, airy aspect. The promenade is popular with joggers, skaters, cyclists and walkers all year round.

Barceloneta Beaches

The walk starts with the 2km (1¼-mile) **Platja de Sant Sebastià ❶** and **Platja de la Barceloneta ❷** by the fishermen's quarter *(see p.59)*. Before

the regeneration, this was where *xiringüítos* (shack-like beach cafés) drew Barcelonans on summer evenings and at weekends, where they would eat fresh fish and sift the sand through their toes. Closest to the city centre, these busy beaches still attract the crowds, and have good facilities.

Just to the northeast of Barceloneta is the **Parc de la Barceloneta ❸**, with the skeleton of an old gasometer, a Modernista warehouse, and a water tower by the Modernista architect Domènech i Estapà. Contrasting with these are the modern buildings of the Hospital del Mar. By the hospital, just before the Port Olímpic, walk down to the lower, beach level of the promenade, where there are several bars with sofas. **Bestial**, see ⑪① *(p.67)*, is one of the coolest, with 'insects' crawling over its glass entrance.

Above from far left: busy beach; lifeguard; sandy cycle ride; sea kayaking equipment.

Below: beach shots.

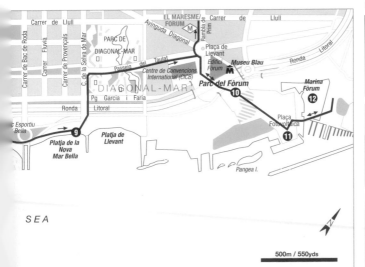

SEA

500m / 550yds

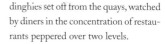

Parc de la Diagonal Mar

This immense space encapsulates the city's desire to be at the forefront of sustainable architecture. It has defined areas – a children's play area, a raised walkway over water, a lake with sculptures that spray water, curved tubular structures, a central plaza – all linked by a common element: water.

Below: Rambla del Poble Nou.

Port Olímpic

From anywhere on the beach, the **Port Olímpic ❹** (Olympic Port) is a beacon, pinpointed by Barcelona's tallest building, the Hotel Arts *(see p.115)*, designed by Bruce Graham (architect of Chicago's Sears Tower and Hancock Building) and by its neighbour, the MAPFRE building, housing offices. Beside them is a giant, glinting, woven-copper fish, *Pez y Esfera* (Fish and Sphere) by the architect Frank Gehry, who is best known for the Bilbao Guggenheim.

The port they overlook was built purely for leisure. Each of its quays is named after a specific wind – *Mestral*, *Xaloc* and *Gregal* (Mistral, West Wind and Northeast Wind). Yachts and

dinghies set off from the quays, watched by diners in the concentration of restaurants peppered over two levels.

Beyond the Port

Paella is a speciality of the beach restaurants alongside **Platja de Nova Icària ❺**, the next stretch of beach. Behind them is the Parc del Port Olímpic, a memento of the Olympics. In Plaça dels Campions (Champions' Square) are the names of the 257 gold medallists, as well as the hand prints of the footballer Pele, cyclist Eddie Merx, chess champion Gary Kasparov and other sporting stars.

The next strip of beach is **Platja del Bogatell ❻**, hidden from the upper promenade by embankments. Your walk here could also be rewarded by lunch at the family-run Xiringuíto Escribà *(see p.120)*.

POBLE NOU

Just before the Mar Bella yacht club, a line of metal poles leads inland to the **Rambla del Poble Nou ❼**, a good place for lunch or a pit stop. Try a refreshing, tiger-nut *orxata* or an ice cream at **El Tio Che**, see ⑪②, on the corner of Carrer del Joncar.

This is the heart of the Poble Nou district, which used to be known for its textile production. Today, the factories have been replaced by design studios, modern office towers and apartment buildings. Gentrification of the area is ongoing, spreading north and west until it eventually merges into Avinguda Diagonal.

DIAGONAL MAR

Back on the beach is **Platja de la Mar Bella ⑧**, with a sports centre behind it, and the Oca Mar restaurant *(see p.120)* on the jetty that divides it from **Platja de la Nova Mar Bella ⑨**.

Here an urban rebirth has taken place at Diagonal Mar, a hi-tech residential and commercial neighbourhood that has brought Avinguda Diagonal, which slices diagonally through the Eixample, down to the coast. The focus of the development is the **Parc del Fòrum ⑩**, a seafront esplanade encompassing a series of buildings and amenities that stage a wide range of events, entertainments and conventions.

The landmark triangular Fòrum Building, by architects Jacques Herzog and Pierre de Meuron became home to the **Museu Blau** (Blue Museum; tel: 93 256 60 02; www.museuzoologia. bcn.es; Tue–Sun 10am–8pm; charge) in 2011. Spanning two floors, this innovative attraction takes you on a journey through the history of life on earth and is a celebration of natural sciences using interactive and audio-visual resources.

Head now towards **Plaça Fotovoltaica ⑪**, the location of a football-pitch-sized sun-catcher, with a startling skewed roof of solar panels. The indoor and outdoor auditoria are both spectacular venues for concerts.

A last stop before catching the metro or a tram (line 4) at El Maresme/ Fòrum back to the city centre is the **Marina Fòrum ⑫**, the latest harbour on this burgeoning leisure coast.

Above from left: Frank Gehry's woven-copper *Pez y Esfera*; beach loungers; reflection of the Hotel Arts in the MAPFRE building; the Fòrum Building.

Just for Joggers
The Passeig Marítim is ideal for joggers. On the far side of Port Olímpic markers are posted for a 1.5km (1-mile) jog.

Food and Drink 🍴

① BESTIAL
Carrer de Ramon Trias i Fargas 2–4; tel: 93 224 04 07; www.bestialdeltragaluz.com; Mon–Thur 1–3.45pm, Fri–Sat 1–3.45pm, 8pm–12.30am, Sun 1–4.30pm, 8–11.30pm; €€
A trendy place with a multi-level beach-side terrace. Minimal decor and fine Italian-inspired rice and pasta.

② EL TIO CHE
Rambla del Poble Nou 44–6; tel: 93 309 18 72; www.eltioche.es; summer daily 10am–10pm, winter Tue–Sun 10am–2pm, 5–10pm; €
Operating on this site since 1933, this bar has the city's best ice creams, plus refreshing lemon slush and deliciously rich *orxata*.

Street Furniture

Among the most striking aspects of this city of *diseny* (design) is the carefully conceived street furniture that makes living outdoors so much more compelling. The tradition is strong. There are 1,600 public drinking fountains in the city, some designed to look like the famous Canaletes on La Rambla *(see p.32),* but the new ones around the Fòrum are elegant modern solutions – single corrugated sheets of metal from which water can be drawn. Seating, too, is imaginative. In the centre of the city, there is usually somewhere to sit, with single seats laid out as if in a domestic setting. Around Diagonal Mar new seats are arranged in pairs and threes beneath lamps, like sofas in a drawing room, giving the seafront a sociable air.

THE EIXAMPLE

The showcase for Gaudí and the Modernista architects, the Eixample was laid out on a strict grid traversed by wide avenues. Today the fantastic facades compete for attention with stylish designer shops and chic locals.

DISTANCE 2km (1½ miles)
TIME 3 hours
START/END Passeig de Gràcia
POINTS TO NOTE

Expect queues at Gaudí's Casa Batlló and La Pedrera – book online for both or try to get there early. Note that from the end of this walk, it is only about 15 minutes' walk to the Sagrada Familia *(see p.72)*.

The Eixample (Extension) was laid out in 1860 in a grid designed by Ildefons Cerdà i Sunyer. Each block had distinct 'cut-off' corners, which offered great opportunity for a newly rich bourgeoisie to build showy homes. It is the district where there is the greatest concentration of buildings designed for domestic purposes by Antoni Gaudí and the Modernistas *(see p.22)*, who shared the belief in craftsmanship and the importance of detail, employing

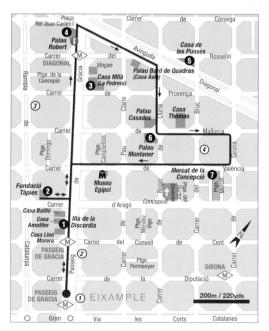

masons, ceramicists, stained-glass specialists and workers in bronze and iron to transform their designs into reality.

ILLA DE LA DISCORDIA

The tour starts at the Passeig de Gràcia metro. Note that there are some good tapas bars on this broad avenue, see ⑪① and ⑪②. Rambla de Catalunya, west of and parallel to Gràcia, is also very civilised, with pavement cafés and bars including **La Bodegueta**, see ⑪③.

Unmissable on the western side of Passeig de Gràcia, between Carrer del Consell de Cent and Carrer d'Aragó at Nos 35–43, is a trilogy of diverse Modernista works, known as **Illa de la Discordia ❶** (Block of Discord), each striking in its own way.

Casas Lleó Morera and Amatller

On the southern corner of the block, at No. 35, is the privately owned **Casa Lleó Morera** (closed to the public), by Lluís Domènech i Montaner, the architect most renowned for his Palau de la Música Catalana *(see p.46)*. The name comes from the words for 'lions' and 'mulberry trees', both elements used in the decoration. The building is distinguished by its fanciful ovoid towers.

Domènech i Montaner mentored Josep Puig i Cadafalch (1867–1957), architect of the next building in the trio: the Dutch-gabled, tiled **Casa Amatller**, three houses further on. The ground-floor entrance, where the caretaker's office contains one of the finest stained-glass windows of the Modernista era is open to visitors (free). There is also a

gallery displaying temporary exhibitions. The house was occupied by the Amatller family (a chocolate-making dynasty) after its completion in 1900.

Casa Batlló

Next door is Gaudí's **Casa Batlló** (tel: 93 216 03 06; www. casabatllo.es; daily 9am–8pm; allow 20 minutes queuing time; best to book online; charge), with a spectacular blue-green ceramic facade, sensuously curving windows and scale-like roof reminiscent of a sea monster (some suggest it depicts St George, patron saint of Barcelona, and the dragon). The house was built for textile baron Josep Batlló, from 1902–6, and its apartments, attic and roof are all now open to visitors.

FUNDACIÓ TÀPIES

After the Block of Discord, turn left into Carrer d'Aragó. At No. 255, on the

Above from far left: on the roof of Casa Batlló; Casa Amatller; stylish Eixample shopper; Modernista architecture, inspired by nature.
Opposite: rooftop features, La Pedrera; Casa Batlló by night.

Modernista Route
Purchase a copy of the *Ruta del Modernisme* guide in one of the three Modernisme centres, tourist outlets and some bookshops for the low-down on all 115 identified sites in the city and beyond, including restaurants and bars, with discount vouchers (www.rutadel modernisme.com).

Food and Drink 🍴

① DIVINUS
Passeig de Gràcia 28; tel: 93 225 81 88; www.restaurante divinus.com; Sun–Thur 7.30am–1.30am, Fri–Sat 9am–2am; €€
In a large, two-storey space, this excellent bar-restaurant has a slick modern feel. Traditional cooking, plus a great range of tapas.

② TAPA TAPA
Passeig de Gràcia 44; tel: 93 488 33 69; www.angrup.com; Mon–Thur 7.45am–1.30am, Fri 7.45am–2am, Sat 8.30am–2am, Sun 9.30am–1am; €€
Over 80 different tapas available in this gastronomic wonder house.

③ LA BODEGUETA
Rambla de Catalunya 100; tel: 93 215 48 94; daily 7.30am–1.30am; €€
Old-fashioned bodega with big barrels and marble tables. Rough red wine accompanies *tacos de manchego* and *jamón serrano*.

north side of the street, crowned by a twisted metal sculpture entitled *Niévol i Cadira* (Cloud and Chair), is the **Fundació Tàpies ❷** (tel: 93 487 03 15; www.fundaciotapies.org; Tue–Sun 10am–7pm). Established in 1984 by the artist Antoni Tàpies (1923–2012) and recently renovated, the foundation is part gallery – showing work by Tàpies and temporary exhibitions – and part study centre, with a smart library. It is housed in a building designed in 1880 by Lluís Domènech i Montaner for his brother's publishing company.

LA PEDRERA

Head back down Carrer d'Aragó to the Passeig de Gràcia. Cross the road and walk to the corner of Carrer de Provença, and **Casa Milà ❸** (tel: 93 484 59 00; www.fundaciocaixacata lunya.org; daily Mar–Oct 10am–8pm, Nov–Feb 10am–6.30pm; charge), commonly called 'La Pedrera' (the stone quarry), after its rippling grey stone facade. Begun in 1901, this extraordi-

nary edifice – Gaudí's most prominent private building – was a controversial project: an eight-storey apartment block devoid of straight lines, set around two inner courtyards. Gaudí put the city's first underground carriage park in the basement and sculpted a roof of evil-looking chimneys, inspired by medieval knights, that were dubbed *espantabruixes*, or 'witch-scarers'.

After years of neglect the building was rescued when Unesco declared it of world-heritage importance, and the Caixa de Catalunya savings bank undertook its restoration. The courtyard, attic (housing an exhibition on Gaudí's work, and of note for its fine parabolic arches), rooftop decorated with *trencadís* (mosaic of broken tiles) and a show flat, in which everything is carefully designed in the Modernista style, can all be visited. There is also a separate exhibition space for temporary shows on the first floor.

North of La Pedrera
Just beyond La Pedrera, at Passeig de Gràcia 96, is **Vinçon**, a leading interior

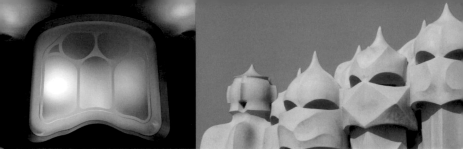

design store, selling everything from stylish stationery and retro toys to furniture and fabrics; exhibitions are also held here. Go upstairs to appreciate the building, which was once the home of the artist Ramón Casas (1866–1932).

Nearby, at Plaça del Rei Joan Carles I, **Palau Robert ❹** houses an information centre for Catalonia. Exhibitions are held here, and there is a pleasant peaceful garden.

AVINGUDA DIAGONAL

Turn right, onto Avinguda Diagonal, which cuts the Eixample diagonally and runs down to the sea. On the right, at No. 373, is **Palau Baró de Quadras**, built in 1904 by Puig i Cadafalch and now home to **Casa Àsia** (tel: 93 238 73 37; www.casaasia.es; Mon–Sat 10am–8pm, Sun 10am–2pm; exhibitions closed Mon; free) a cultural centre focusing on Asia and the Asian Pacific through exhibitions and a library. There is a beautiful little courtyard and lovely glass balconies on the second floor, a café, and roof terrace.

As you continue down the Diagonal, look out, two blocks along, for Puig i Cadafalch's neo-Gothic **Casa de les Punxes ❺** (House of the Spikes).

Modernista Landmarks

At this point turn right down Carrer de Roger de Llúria. At the corner of Carrer de Mallorca, on the northern side, is the **Palau Casades**, now housing the Il.lustre Col.legi d'Advocats (Law College). On the south side is **Palau Montaner ❻** (guided tours only

Sat–Sun, tour in English Sat 10.30am; charge) with attractive tiled eaves and a mosaic exterior. Designed by Domènech i Montaner as a private home for his brother – the whole family lived here from 1893 until 1939 – it now shelters the government of Madrid in Barcelona.

Domènech i Montaner also built **Casa Thomas** at Carrer de Mallorca, 291–3, a few steps down on the left, and now occupied by **El Favorita**, a modern furniture designers. (You can walk in and admire the building.)

Continue a block to Carrer de Girona, then turn right and right again to the 19th-century glass-and-iron **Mercat de la Concepció ❼** (Carrer d'Aragó 313–17; Mon, Sat 8am–3pm, Tue–Fri 8am–8pm; *see p.14*), selling all manner of foodstuffs and with a couple of stalls where you can get a drink and a snack. Alternatively, back on Carrer de Valencia turn first right into Carrer de Bruc for lunch at **Asador de Burgos**, see ⑪④. On the way back to Passeig de Gràcia you will pass the **Museu Egipci** (Carrer de València 284; tel: 93 488 01 88; www.museu egipci.com; Mon–Sat 10am–8pm, Sun 10am–2pm; charge) an important private collection of Egyptian artefacts including mummies, statuary, funereal implements, ceramics and jewellery.

Fashion Tips

Some of Barcelona's key designers are based in the Eixample. One of the best known is Antonio Miró, whose shop is at Carrer del Consell de Cent 349. Other places to visit include Adolfo Dominguez (Passeig de Gràcia 32) and On Land (Carrer de València 273), the latter with clothes for both men and women from young and established designers including Josep Abril. Camiseria Pons is attractively located in a Modernista building at Carrer Gran de Gràcia 49. Salvador Bachiller (Carrer de Mallorca 243) has been creating accessories and travel goods since 1942 but is still on trend.

Food and Drink 🍴

④ **ASADOR DE BURGOS**

Carrer de Bruc 118; tel: 93 207 31 60; www.asadorde burgos.es; daily 1–4pm, Wed–Sat also 8pm–midnight; €€
Traditional place where meat is grilled in an oak wood adobe oven.

SAGRADA FAMÍLIA
AND PARK GÜELL

No visit to Barcelona is complete without a tour of the buildings of the great Modernista architect Antoni Gaudí. His stunning Sagrada Família is an essential visit, and can be combined with a trip to his house–museum in the fantasy-style Park Güell, nesting high above the city.

DISTANCE 3km (2 miles)

TIME 4 hours

START Sagrada Família

END Park Güell

POINTS TO NOTE

This is a two-destination tour, and you can buy a combined ticket for both the Sagrada Família and the Casa-Museu Gaudí in Park Güell at either place.

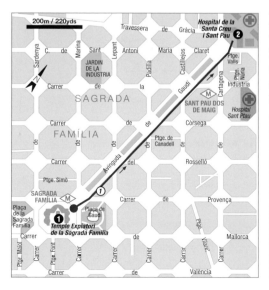

Start the day with the astonishing, unfinished temple of Antoni Gaudí (1852–1926), easily reached by metro (Sagrada Família station on lines L2 and L5). There are many places to eat on the Avinguda de Gaudí; try the traditional **Catalan La Llesca**, see ⑪①.

SAGRADA FAMÍLIA

After Gaudí had completed his last commission, Casa Milà (La Pedrera; *see p.70*), in 1910, he devoted the remaining 16 years of his life to the **Temple Expiatori de la Sagrada Família ❶** (Carrer de Mallorca 401; tel: 93 207 30 31; www.sagradafamilia.org; daily Apr–Sept 9am–8pm, Oct–Mar 9am–6pm; charge; guided tours

Food and Drink 🍴

① LA LLESCA

Avinguda de Gaudí 12; tel: 93 455 31 30; daily 1–4pm, 8.30–11.30pm; €

This family-run Catalan restaurant is good value. It offers speciality dishes such as braised artichokes; *escalivada* – grilled vegetables served with meat or as a starter; and squid Catalan-style. It also serves the toasts called *llescas*, which give the restaurant its name.

available daily, in English; reduced price combined ticket option with Casa-Museu Gaudí in Park Güell). Gaudí spent his last 10 years working unpaid from a hut on site. He lived extremely modestly, putting all his money and energy into his building, until his death in 1926.

Existing Facades

Before entering, it is worth circling the unfinished building to get an idea of its layout. The austere west front was completed in the 1980s with statues by local artist, Josep Maria Subirachs, and by the Japanese sculptor, Etsuro Soto. The only facade Gaudí completed is the eastern one dedicated to the Nativity, with three doorways: Faith, Hope and Charity, and four coloured, tentacled towers, one of which has an internal lift to take visitors skywards.

Work in Progress

Part of the fascination lies in watching the builders and craftsmen going about their work. In 2010 the main nave was finally covered, resplendent with tree-like columns and dazzling roof. The church was consecrated by Pope Benedict XVI on 7 November 2010. At 110m (360ft) in length, the Sagrada Família will eventually be 27m (87ft) longer than the city's cathedral and nearly twice the height, with a main tower rising to 198m (650ft), half as high again as those that are already here. The church has eight spires, with Gaudí's original plans showing 18. Completion is currently set for 2030 – the once preferred date of 2026,

commemorating the centenary of Gaudí's death, now looking increasingly unlikely.

Crypt

The crypt where Gaudí is buried also houses the museum that shows how he envisaged the finished temple, and how his ideas often changed. Controversy over the final design still rages as to whether it will live up to Gaudí's dream.

HOSPITAL DE LA SANTA CREU

On leaving the Sagrada Família, stroll up Avinguda de Gaudí on the north side of the temple. This anarchic diagonal avenue – Gaudí disliked the rigidity of the Eixample – leads to the **Hospital de la Santa Creu i Sant Pau** ❷ (Carrer de Sant Antoni María Claret 167; tel: tel: 93 317 76 52; guided tours in English daily 10am, 11am, noon, 1pm; charge).

Designed by Lluís Domènech i Montaner, and begun in 1902, the hospital is a fine Modernista work, with separate pavilions connected by underground walkways, in the style of a pleasant garden city, to speed the recovery of its patients. It is now a Unesco World Heritage Site.

PARK GÜELL

It is now time to progress to **Park Güell** ❸ (Carrer d'Olot; daily 10am–sunset; free). There are several ways of reaching it from the Sagrada Família: hop on the tourist bus outside

Above from far left: view of the Sagrada Família from across the city at Montjuïc *(see p.75)*, showing a diver in the 1992 Olympic Games; the church's eastern facade, which was finished by Gaudí; spire detail; the construction continues.

Opposite and below: details from the Sagrada Família and Park Güell.

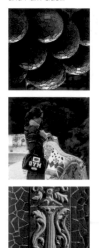

Above from left:
Casa-Museu Gaudí;
mosaic sculpture;
Montjuïc's Caixa-
Forum; Fundació
Joan Miró.

Park Plots
Only three plots for
Güell's planned
garden city were
sold. One was
bought by Gaudí
himself and is now
the Casa-Museu; the
other two were sold
to the Trias family,
who still own them.

the church; take the metro to Lesseps
(*as shown on pull-out map*), then walk
uphill 1.2km (³⁄₄ mile) or take the No.
24 bus; or take No. 92 bus from outside the Hospital de la Santa Creu i
Sant Pau. Alternatively, hail a taxi.

Background
The site was originally owned by
Gaudí's patron, the affluent industri-
alist Eusebi Güell, who had wanted
to create a garden city of houses in the
English style here – hence the English
spelling of 'park'. The project never
came to full fruition, and in 1922 the
Güell family donated the park to the
city instead.

The Park
The main entrance is flanked by two
whimsical pavilions designed by
Gaudí. The one on the left is a shop,

while the one on the right houses an
exhibition giving the background to
the construction of the park.

A double staircase, presided over by
a magnificent tile-mosaic salamander,
leads up to the park's main feature, a
two-tiered plaza. The lower part is a
hypostyle hall, originally intended to
be the market hall for the estate.
Framing the plaza is a wavy, tile-
mosaic parapet from where there is a
grand view out over the city. This
long, colourful, undulating bench –
which, with the salamander, is the
most photographed aspect of the park
– was actually the work not of Gaudí
but his assistant, Josep Jujol i Gibert.

Take time to wander the pathways
that wind through the park. Some are
in the form of extraordinary viaducts
supported by twisting stone pillars.
Green parakeets can often be spotted
darting in and out of the palm trees.

Casa-Museu Gaudí
In 1906, Gaudí bought the home of
architect Francesc Berenguer, to the
right of the park entrance. The sweet
building, like something out of a fairy-
tale, is now the **Casa-Museu Gaudí**
(tel: 93 219 38 11; www.casamuseu
gaudi.org; daily Apr–Sept 10am–
7.45pm, Oct–Mar 10am–5.45pm;
charge). On three floors, it still houses
furniture from the architect's time,
including his bed, *prie-dieu* and crucifix.

Return to the centre on bus No. 24,
or from Lesseps metro. If you are still
feeling energetic, you could walk down
to Gràcia for a look at Gaudí's Casa
Vicens (*see p.84*).

MONTJUÏC

Named after a Jewish cemetery, Barcelona's southern hill is home to the region's most notable art collection, a scattering of buildings erected for the 1992 Olympics, the world-class Fundació Joan Miró and the fun Poble Espanyol.

The buildings that were erected for the 1992 Olympic Games were the last in a line of attractions to be located on the 213m (700ft) high hill of Montjuïc. The majority of the grand exhibition halls and cultural palaces here are remnants of the city's previous key cultural event, the Universal Exhibition of 1929.

But the hill has long featured in the city's history. Its stone was quarried to build the cathedral, and its castle, which has a wonderful 360-degree panorama, has witnessed all the triumphs and cruelties of the city's history.

Ongoing plans to improve and develop the Montjuïc hill include a new walkway, the Passeig del Cims (Promenande of the Peaks), terraced to make climbing the steep incline easier.

PLAÇA D'ESPANYA

The best way to approach Montjuïc, to fully appreciate its grandeur, is from the **Plaça d'Espanya ❶**, served by metro lines 1 and 3. Beside the square is the neo-Mudéjar **Las Arenas**, a vast bullring built in 1899 and now home to the **Arenas de Barcelona** (www.arenasdebarcelona.com), a shopping, cultural and recreational facility. Opened in 2011 the centre comprises shops, restaurants, cinemas and even an out-

> **DISTANCE** 5km (3 miles)
> **TIME** 5 hours
> **START** Plaça d'Espanya
> **END** Paral.lel metro
> **POINTS TO NOTE**
> You will not be able to do justice to all Montjuïc's attractions in a day, so decide which elements you want to see before setting out. The hill is steep and the roads meander; take the bus or funicular *(see right)*, to save energy.

door running track. Atop the building is a domed theatre and concert hall, the Cúpola de las Arenas. On the fourth floor is the Museu del Rock (tel: 93 426 50 54; www.museudelrock.com; Tue–Sun 10am–10pm; charge) with six galleries of memorabilia of rock music from its origins to the present day.

UP TOWARDS THE HILL

Walk up **Avinguda de la Reina Maria Cristina** through Lluís Domènech i Montaner's copies of Venice's campanile, which flagged the triumphant approach to the 1929 exhibition. On either side of this esplanade are the vast trade fair halls of Barcelona's **Fira de Barcelona**, some of which have been doing useful service since 1929.

No Bullfighting
Bullfighting in Catalonia has been banned and the last *corrida* in Barcelona was held in September 2011.

Funicular and Bus
One way of getting up and down Montjuïc is to use the funicular than runs from Paral.lel metro to just above the Fundació Joan Miró. From there the *teleféric* cable car ascends to the castle. The hop-on, hop-off tourist bus from Plaça d'Espanya to the castle runs every 40 minutes from mid-June to mid-September (weekends only in winter), stopping at all the major sights mentioned in this route on the way. Alternatively, hop in a taxi to take you from sight to sight.

Above from left:
Pavelló Mies van der Rohe; statue at the pavilion; decorative dome at the Palau Nacional; exterior of the Palau Nacional.

'Barcelona' Chair
Mies van der Rohe designed his now-iconic chrome-and-leather 'Barcelona' chair as a throne for the Spanish king and queen on their visit to the 1929 Universal Exhibition.

Font Màgica de Montjuïc

At the top of the avenue, reached by outdoor escalators (if they are working), is the **Font Màgica de Montjuïc ❷** (Magic Fountain; tel: 93 256 44 30; May–Sept Thur–Sun 9–11.30pm, Oct–May Fri–Sat 7–9pm; free), designed by Carles Buïgas in 1929. Rising to 50m (164ft), it is magnificent after dark, when it is lit by 4,500 coloured lights and dances to music from Beethoven to Hollywood film tunes.

Museu d'Arqueologia and Around

If you were to head left at this point, you would soon reach the **Mercat de les Flors**, a complex of theatres that includes the **Institut del Teatre** and **Teatre Lliure**, which puts on a broad range of stage productions, and has a good restaurant, see ⑪①.

Nearby is the **Museu d'Arqueologia** (Passeig de Santa Madrona 39–41; tel: 93 423 21 49; www.mac.cat; Tue–Sat 9.30am–7pm, Sun 10am–2.30pm; charge). Built for the 1929 exhibition as the Palace of Graphic Arts, it houses archaeological finds from the city, from the Graeco-Roman trading post at Empúries and from the Iberian settlement at Ullastret on the Costa Brava.

Opposite is a public garden leading to the open-air **Teatre Grec**. Also built for the 1929 exhibition and set in a former stone quarry, it is used for plays and concerts in the summer, as part of the two-month Festival del Grec (tel: 93 316 10 00; www.grec.bcn.cat).

Pavelló Mies van der Rohe

Back at the Font Màgica, just to its right, on Avinguda de Francesc Ferrer

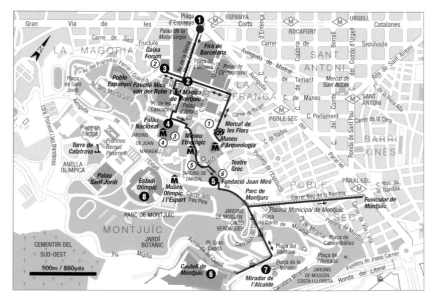

i Guàrdia, is the **Pavelló Mies van der Rohe** (tel: 93 423 40 16; daily 10am–8pm; charge). It was designed by Bauhaus director Mies van der Rohe as the German Pavilion, a reception area for the 1929 exhibition, and is remarkable for its spare lines in sleek marble and glass, complemented by a tranquil small pool. The original pavilion was demolished after the Universal Exhibition, but it was rebuilt in 1986 to celebrate the centenary of the designer's birth.

CaixaForum

Opposite the pavilion is a Modernista factory, Casaramona, built in 1911 by Josep Puig i Cadafalch. Redesigned by Arata Isozaki as the **CaixaForum ❸** (tel: 93 476 86 00; www.fundacio. lacaixa.es; daily 10am–8pm, some areas closed Mon; free), it is one of the most exciting cultural spaces in the city, staging exhibitions across its four galleries, plus concerts, films and talks. It is also home to a permanent exhibition recounting the history of the building, a media centre, a bookshop, and a good café, see ⑪②.

PALAU NACIONAL

The next main sight en route is the **Palau Nacional ❹**, the formidable neoclassical palace that dominates the fountain and the approach up Avinguda de la Reina Cristina. The palace is home to the **Museu Nacional d'Art de Catalunya** (**MNAC;** tel: 93 622 03 76; www.mnac.cat; Tue–Sat 10am–7pm, Sun 10am–2.30pm;

charge except first Sun of month; tickets are valid for two days), a repository of Catalan, Renaissance, Gothic and modern art, and, most notably, the finest collection of Romanesque art in the world.

The Collection

The most striking of its lower rooms, devoted to Romanesque decoration,

---

Food and Drink

① **EL LLIURE**

Teatre Lliure, Passeig Santa Madrona; tel: 93 237 12 43; Tue–Fri 1–4pm, and before and until two hours after performances; €€
This theatre restaurant has an innovative menu for indoor and outdoor meals.

② **LAIE-CAIXAFORUM**

Avinguda del Marqués de Comillas 6–8; tel: 93 476 86 69; Sun–Fri 10am–6pm, Sat 10am–10pm; €
A daily set menu, plus salads, sandwiches, pastries and juices.

Poble Espanyol

If you continue walking up Avinguda de Francesc Ferrer i Guàrdia from the CaixaForum, you will reach the Poble Espanyol or Spanish Village (tel: 93 508 63 00; www.poble-espanyol.com; Mon 9am–8pm, Tue–Thur and Sun 9am–midnight, Fri 9am–3am, Sat 9am–4am; charge), one of the city's most popular sites, attracting 1.5 million, mostly Spanish, visitors a year. Some 120 buildings represent architecture from across Spain, from Moorish Andalusia to the rugged Basque country, in styles from the 12th to the 19th centuries. The complex was designed for the 1929 exhibition and has since become a leisure centre and a 'City of Artisans', where you can see glassmakers, weavers, potters and ironmongers at work in some 40 craft workshops, plus 22 craft shops. Its restaurants are popular in the evenings, and night spots include the Tablao de Carmen, with a flamenco show, and a hip club, La Terraza, with open-air dancing in summer.

Above from left:
Fundació Joan Miró;
Inmaculada Concepción by Francisco de Zurbarán, at the MNAC; Torre de Calatrava; cable cars.

are those containing wall paintings peeled from the apses of remote Pyrenean churches in the early 20th century, transported here by mule train and restored. These are complemented by crucifixes, altarpieces and caskets.

The collection of Gothic and Renaissance art is less complete, although Catalonia's Gothic masters Jaume Huguet, Bernat Martorell and Lluís Borrassa are represented. The Baroque assemblage has been augmented by the addition of the Thyssen collection that was formerly housed in the Pedralbes monastery *(see p.82)*.

The museum's Catalan collection includes 19th- and 20th-century work by Casas, Rusiñol, Gargallo and Fortuny, as well as decorative art from Modernista interiors, including fur-niture by Gaudí and Jujol. One room has nine works by Picasso; another is dedicated to Catalan photography, with a small collection of prints including a couple of iconic pictures from the Civil War. These displays are further enhanced by a selection of paintings from the collection of Carmen Thyssen-Bornemisza.

In addition to the galleries, the museum houses a large concert hall, an open-plan area with comfortable sofas (on the first floor beneath the building's dome), a café, see ⑪③, and a smarter restaurant, **Oleum**, see ⑪④.

FUNDACIÓ JOAN MIRÓ

The next suggested main stop on the route is the Fundació Joan Miró, which can be reached by turning right out of the Palau Nacional and walking up the hill. This takes you past the **Museu Etnològic** (Passeig de Santa Madrona; tel: 93 424 68 07; www.museuetnologic.bcn.es; closed for renovation, due to open 2013), the city's Ethnology Museum. Turn into the lovely **Jardins de Laribal** (10am–sunset; free), where the **El Font del Gat** café-restaurant, see ⑪⑤, makes for a pleasant pit stop.

A short walk further is the **Fundació Joan Miró ❺** (tel: 93 329 19 08; www.fundaciomiro-bcn.org; Tue–Sat July–Sept 10am–8pm, Oct–June 10am–7pm, year-round Thur until 9.30pm, Sun 10am–2.30pm; charge), in a building by architect Josep Lluís Sert (1902–83) to showcase the work of the painter Joan Miró (1893–1983) and opened in 1975.

Montjuïc's Gardens

There are a number of gardens on Montjuïc – the formal, French-style Jardins de Joan Maragall form the grounds of the Palauet Albéniz, while the Jardins de Mossèn Cinto Verdaguer are in the English country-house style. The 14-hectare (35-acre) Jardí Botànic, between the Olympic Stadium and the castle, is a sustainable garden showcasing plants from across the Mediterranean. Jardins de Mossèn Costa i Llobrera, on the south side of the hill and sloping towards the sea, was once a strategic defence point for the city, the Buenavista battery. The cactus garden reopened in 2011 after years of renovation. It has cacti from across the world, from Mexico, Bolivia, Africa and California.

The gallery houses a large and excellent collection of Miró's work, including his trademark primary-colour sculptures out on the roof. Concerts are held here regularly, and there is also a pleasant restaurant, see ⑦⑥.

CASTELL DE MONTJUÏC

From the gallery, walk five minutes up Avinguda de Mirmar to the **funicular station**. From here, you can either take the *teleféric* cable car or a bus for the five-minute ride up to the **Castell de Montjuïc ❻** (daily Apr–Sept 9am–9pm, Oct–Mar 9am–7pm; free). Built in 1640 during the Harvesters' Revolt the castle was redesigned in the reign of Felipe V. In 1939, at the end of the Civil War, it was used as a prison and execution ground. There are plans to develop the castle site in the future, possibly as a research centre promoting peace.

From just below the castle, by the **Mirador de l'Alcalde ❼** and the statue of Sardana dancers, the *teleféric* will take you back to the funicular and Paral.lel metro, or you can get a bus back to Plaça d'Espanya.

OLYMPIC SITES

If you want to admire the legacy of the 1992 Olympic Games, take the bus that runs between the castle and the Plaça d'Espanya, and get off at the **Estadi Olímpic ❽** (Olympic Stadium) stop. What you see today is the remodelled 1929 stadium with recent alterations made for the 20th European Athletics Championships, held here in 2010. It also hosts concerts, and has featured artists such as Bruce Springsteen, Madonna and Coldplay.

Beside the stadium is the innovative **Museu Olímpic i de l'Esport** (tel: 93 292 53 79; www.museuolimpicbnc.cat; Apr–Sept Tue–Sat 10am–8pm, Oct–Mar 10am–6pm, Sun 10am–2.30pm all year; charge). On display are items from the 1992 Olympics and lots of interactive items and memorabilia from the world of sport.

Just beyond it are the striking **Palau Sant Jordi** indoor sports stadium and the **Bernat Picornell** swimming pool *(see margin)*. The 188m (616ft) **Torre de Calatrava** communications tower rises from the **Plaça d'Europa**, from where there are fine views to the south.

High Divers

Up the road from the funicular station are the municipal baths, Piscines Bernat Picornell (Avinguda de l'Estadi 30; tel: 93 423 40 41; outdoor pool: June–Sept Mon–Sat 9am–9pm, Sun 9am–8pm, Oct–May Mon–Sat 10am–6pm, Sun 10am–4pm; indoor pool longer hours; charge), built for the 1992 Olympic diving events. With precipitous tiered seating, they have fabulous views of the city. Films are sometimes shown here as part of the Grec festival.

Food and Drink 🍴

③ CÚBIC CAFETERIA
Palau Nacional; tel: 93 622 03 60; Tue–Sat 9am–6.30pm, Sun–Mon 9am–4pm; €
A slice of of the Oval Hall is taken up with this straightforward café, which serves sandwiches and pastries.

④ OLEUM
Palau Nacional; tel: 93 289 06 79; daily 1–4pm; €€
With panoramic views reflected in its mirrored ceiling, this smart restaurant serves Mediterranean food, using top-quality produce.

⑤ EL FONT DEL GAT
Passeig de Santa Madrona 28; tel: 93 289 04 04; Tue–Sun 1–4pm; €€
In the middle of the formal gardens, this café restaurant offers home-made ices and sorbets, and a good fixed-price lunch menu.

⑥ BAR RESTAURANT
Fundació Miró, Avinguda de Miramar 1; tel: 93 329 07 68; Tue–Sat 1–3.45pm, Sun 1–2.30pm (bar only); €
Lovely restaurant with an outdoor courtyard and good staples such as pasta plus local dishes including an aromatic rabbit stew.

BARÇA

One of the world's richest football clubs, with about 170,000 members, and Barcelona's top team, Barça infuses the city with pride. Its museum, the focus of this short tour, is one of the most popular in the city.

DISTANCE 1km (½ mile)

TIME 2 hours

START/END Palau Reial metro

POINTS TO NOTE

This is a good family outing: it is relatively brief, with just a short walk to the stadium from the metro, and not expensive. It could be combined with a visit to Palau Reial *(see p.83).*

More than a Club

The Barça slogan, *'més que un club'* (more than a club), reflects the club's place in the cultural history of Catalonia. It presents Barça as the defender of rights and freedoms, a reputation earned during the Franco years, when matches against Madrid were notoriously weighted in the capital's favour. Today, Barça's fan base extends well beyond Catalonia, and to show its continued caring side towards the world, it makes a regular contribution to United Nations' humanitarian aid programmes, and players wear the Unicef logo on the back of their shirts.

After the Museu Picasso *(see p.49)*, the museum at Barça football club is the most visited in the city. Fans from all over the world come to see one of Europe's largest stadiums, to wonder at the club's many trophies, watch playbacks, gloat over past glories and stand in the director's box.

Barça matches bring the city to a standstill and have Barcelonans in thrall (note that the city does have another football club, Espanyol, which is based at the RCDE Stadium in the suburb of Cornella de Llobrega.

Getting There

When you step out of the **Palau Reial metro** ❶ on the south side of Avinguda Diagonal, the dome of the stadium is immediately evident behind the massive university car park. It is just a 10-minute walk through the car park to the entrance, where stalls sell souvenir scarves, strips and other memorabilia. But wait till you get inside the wire fence to find the largest collection of memorabilia, in the two-storey **FCBotiga Megastore**.

CAMP NOU STADIUM

The stadium, **Camp Nou** ❷ (Avinguida de Aristides Maillol, Les Corts; tel: 93 496 36 00; www.fcbarcelona.

cat; Apr–Sept Mon–Sat 10am–8pm, Sun 10am–2.30pm, Oct–Mar Mon–Sat 10am–6.30pm, Sun 10am–2.30pm; charge), meaning 'new ground', has been home to the club since 1957. It is the largest constituent part of a sports complex just below the university campus and the smart end of Avinguda Diagonal and can hold around 99,000 spectators.

Basketball, hockey, handball, junior football and ice hockey are also catered for in its neighbouring buildings, the **Miniestadi**, the **Palau Blaugrana** (*blau* translates as blue, *grana* as burgundy: the club colours) and the **Pista de Gel** ice rink.

Tour and Museum

The main ticket office, opposite the store, is where to buy tickets to the **Museu del FC Barcelona** (opening hours as above). The entrance fee includes an audio tour of the dressing rooms, tunnel to the pitch, players' benches, presidential box and press room. The museum has been updated to provide more multimedia experiences but still contains the many trophies Barça has amassed in its long, illustrious history. There is a roll-call of famous players and managers, and action-replay videos. The best part, however, is simply looking out on to the breathtaking arena and imagining the mood during games.

Above from far left: inside the Barça Megastore; supportive flags.

Above: Barça badge; club scarves.

Food and Drink 🍴

There are very few cafés or restaurants in the vicinity of Camp Nou so consider eating elsewhere before your visit or bring a packed lunch with you. The stadium only has basic facilities available for drinks and light snacks.

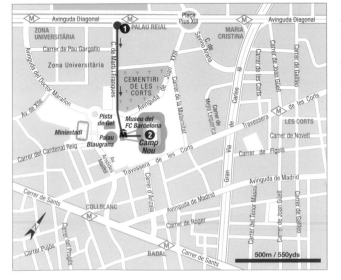

Ticket Sales

Match tickets can be purchased in advance online through the club's website. Same-day tickets can be bought in the stadium's ticket offices on Travessera de les Corts or Avinguda de Joan XXIII. Matches start between 5 and 9pm. *Entrada general* are cheap, top-tier tickets, *Lateral* are mid-priced ones, and *Tribuna* are for covered seats. Note that tickets are scarce for big matches.

PEDRALBES

This tour starts in the genteel suburb of Sarrià, then heads to the atmospheric Gothic monastery of Pedralbes in the hills and, further down, the 20th-century Palau Reial, which has a fabulous ceramics collection.

DISTANCE 2km (1 mile)
TIME 3 hours
START Reina Elisenda FGC station, Sarrià
END Palau Reial metro
POINTS TO NOTE
The FGC train from Plaça de Catalunya takes 10 minutes to Sarrià (bus takes 40 minutes), from where it is a 10-minute walk to the monastery, then 20 minutes on foot to the Palau Reial. Take a bottle of water with you, as there are few cafés en route.

Reina Elisenda FGC station is in the centre of **Sarrià ❶**, once a village, now an atmospheric, sought-after district of Barcelona, with a market, smoky bars and traditional restaurants, see ⑪①. The *barrio* is somewhat reminiscent of a provincial Catalan town, with gardens bursting with bougainvillea, pretty Modernista villas and old-fashioned shops.

THE MONASTERY

From the station, it is a 10-minute walk along Passeig de la Reina Elisenda de Montcada to the gold-stoned **Monestir de Pedralbes ❷** (Baixada del Monestir 9; tel: 93 256 34 34; Apr–Sept Tue–Fri 10am–5pm, Sat 10am–7pm, Sun 10am–8pm, Oct–Mar Tue–Sat 10am– 2pm, Sun 10am–5pm; charge except first Sun of month), accessed up a cobbled lane and through an arch.

The monastery was founded by Queen Elisenda de Montcada, wife of Jaume II (the Just), for nuns of the Order of St Clare. The queen took the vows and retreated here after Jaume's death in 1327. There are still a few nuns living here, but most parts of the monastery are open to visitors as the **Museu Monestir de Pedralbes**.

The three-storey cloister is Catalan-

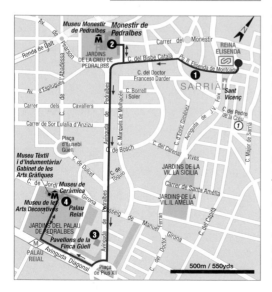

Above from far left:
frescoes by Ferrer
Bassa; cross at the
monastery; statue at
the Palau Reial;
monastery cloisters.

Gothic at its most elegant. In the gardens are fruit trees, and former nuns' cells lead off around the sides.

When the monastery was fully operational, the sick were tended in the infirmary, and four rooms from this part of the complex now contain exhibits on the daily routine of the Poor Clares who lived here. You can visit the refectory where they ate in silence and, beside it, the kitchens.

The Church

Leaving the museum, continue along the side of the building to reach the entrance to the complex's church, a simple Gothic building containing Queen Elisenda's marble tomb. Part of the nave at the back of the church, behind a grille, is used by the few nuns who live in the buildings opposite the old monastery.

FINCA GÜELL

Leave the monastery and walk down Avinguda de Pedralbes for about 10 minutes, past the luxurious (but rather soulless) apartment blocks in this exclusive part of town. Near the bottom, on the former farm estate of Gaudí's patron, Eusabi Güell, you will see, at No. 7, the **Pavellons de la Finca Güell** ❸ (tel: 93 317 76 52; www.rutadel modernisme.com; open for guided visits only; tours in English Sat–Sun 10.15am and 12.15pm; charge) with a magnificent entrance gate, a tortuous iron work by Gaudí featuring a dragon known as the Drac de Pedralbes. One pavilion houses a Ruta del Modernisme information centre *(see margin, p.69)*.

PALAU REIAL

Beyond the Finca, accessed from Avinguda Diagonal, the Renaissance-style **Palau Reial** ❹ (Avinguda Palau Reial de Pedralbes), surrounded by formal Italianate gardens, was built by the city council in 1925 to encourage visits from Alfonso XIII. The king went into exile six years later, but his throne room is still here.

The palace now houses four museums. The **Museu de Ceràmica** (tel: 93 256 34 65; www.museuce ramica.bcn.es; Tue–Sun 10am–6pm; charge except first Sun of month) has a collection that includes Islamic tiles, pottery by Picasso, and modern works. The three other museums, the **Museu de les Arts Decoratives**, the **Museu Tèxtil i d'Indumentària** and the **Gabinet de les Arts Gràfiques** (www.dhub-bcn.cat; hours as for Museu de Ceràmica), will be moved to Les Glòries *(see margin, p.63)* at a future date. Meanwhile they showcase European decorative art and Spanish industrial design, textiles and fashion from the 16th century to the present day, and graphic art and typography.

Return to the city centre via the Palau Reial metro, situated just outside the palace entrance.

Above: details from the Museu de les Arts Decoratives.

Food and Drink

① CASA JOANA

Carrer Major de Sarrià 59, Sarrià; tel: 93 203 10 36; Mon–Sat 1–4pm, 9–11pm; €

Long-established, little-changed place, serving tasty home cooking at good prices. Popular with local families at weekends.

GRÀCIA

Away from the bustle of the town centre, the slightly bohemian neighbourhood of Gràcia offers peaceful streets, some with lovely Modernista facades, intriguing shops and bars, and a sense of community.

DISTANCE 2km (1 mile)

TIME 1hr 30mins

START Fontana metro

END Diagonal metro

POINTS TO NOTE

This is a suggested walk around Gràcia, but there are few key monuments in this area. For ease of walking, the tour starts at the top and goes downhill.

Above: designer fashions *(top)* and accessories *(centre)* on Passeig de Gràcia; sculpture in Plaça del Sol.

Festa Major

For eight days in the middle of August Gràcia's streets and squares are filled with music, parades, cava drinkers and wildly innovative designs, as the residents compete for the title of best decorated street.

Above the Diagonal, beyond the Passeig de Gràcia, the *vila* of Gràcia was, until 1897, a community in its own right. With a reputation for radicalism and a strong identity, it maintains a tradition of artisans and small family businesses. It is full of lovely cafés and bars and attractive little squares.

By day the small shops, boutiques and alternative outlets have a pleasing, quirky, feel but by night, as doors open on bars, restaurants and a couple of small cinemas, as well as a theatre with a strong local reputation, the area has a more vibrant ambience.

CASA VICENS

Start at the **Fontana metro ❶** in **Carrer Gran de Gràcia**, an extension of the Passeig de Gràcia, lined with shops and Modernista apartment blocks and also the location of one of Barcelona's finest fish restaurants, the Galician **Botafumeiro**, see ⑪①. The Modernista facades are even more striking in **Rambla del Prat** (left out of the station, then first right).

At the end of the Rambla turn right, then take the second right down Carrer de les Carolines, and you will see **Casa Vicens ❷**, on the left. This was Antoni Gaudí's first major commission, attained at the age of 32, from a ceramic and tile

manufacturer – as is evident from the colourful facade. Note the highly elaborate fence. Closed to the public, the building has been inhabited by the same family since its completion in 1885.

PLAÇA DEL SOL

Continue across Gran de Gràcia, turn right and zigzag down the small streets, lined with workshops, grocery stores and trendy clothes shops, until you reach **Plaça del Sol ❸**. A favourite spot among students and young people as well as local families, it is lined by cafés, including the ever-popular **Sol Soler**, see ⑪②.

As the evening wears on, the families take their children home, and the square becomes a centre of the area's night-time buzz. Attractive architecture includes the green *esgrafiat* (incised decoration) on the Envalira restaurant, while a Lebanese restaurant in the square is a sign of the growing social mix.

PLAÇA DE LA VILA DE GRÀCIA

Continue down, across the lively Travessera de Gràcia, home to the local market, to Gràcia's main square, **Plaça de la Vila de Gràcia ❹**, formerly called Plaça de Rius I Taulet and renamed in 2009. Highlights include **El Rellotge**, the 1864 town hall clock tower. Like all Gràcia squares, this is a popular place for people to sit and children to play.

Wend your way towards the bottom of Gran de Gràcia and **Casa Fuster ❺** *(see below)*. From here it is just a short walk down to Avinguda Diagonal and the Diagonal metro.

Above from far left: Casa Vicens; taking a stroll in Gràcia.

The Time of Doves Plaça del Diament is the setting for Mercè Rodoredo's 1962 novel of the same name (*The Time of Doves* in English). The book has been translated into more languages than any other Catalan work of literature.

Food and Drink 🍴

① BOTAFUMEIRO
Carrer Gran de Gràcia 81; tel: 93 218 42 30; www.botafumeiro.es; daily 1pm–1am; €€€€
One of the best (and most expensive) fish restaurants in Barcelona. So good even the king has dined here.

② SOL SOLER
Plaça del Sol 21; tel: 93 217 44 40; daily noon–2.30am; €€
This old bodega, in the unofficial centre of the district, has wooden tables and a lively young crowd. Simple food includes couscous, *tortillas* and quiche.

Casa Fuster

At the bottom of Carrer Gran de Gràcia is Casa Fuster, Domènech i Montaner's last building in Barcelona, completed in 1911. Built over six storeys with marble columns and luxuriant stone carving, it was the most expensive private building in the city. For many years the Café Vienès occupied the ground floor, and El Danubio dance hall, a focal point for society, was in the basement. In 2000 the building was purchased by the Hoteles Center company and overhauled as a magnificent 5-star hotel, and the Café Vienès (*illustrated below*) reopened on the ground floor.

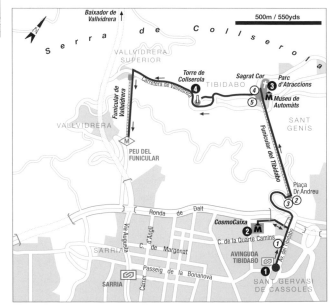

TIBIDABO

The hill that looks down on Barcelona is crowned by a historic amusement park and criss-crossed by walking paths. It is accessible by tram and funicular, with the excellent CosmoCaixa science museum en route.

DISTANCE 10km (6 miles)
TIME 5 hours
START Avinguda Tibidabo FGC
END Plaça de Catalunya
POINTS TO NOTE

Tibidabo funfair is open from March to December only. The best time to visit is late afternoon or early evening, as the sunsets are spectacular. The Tramvia Blau and funicular only run when the Parc d'Atraccions is open.

Above: stained-glass window in the Sagrat Cor church; the Tramvia Blau.

According to the Bible, the Devil took Christ up into 'an exceeding high mountain and sheweth him all the kingdoms of the world, and the glory of them; and saith unto him, All these things *I will give thee [tibi dabo]* if thou wilt fall down and worship me.'

Tibidabo is the 517m (1,700ft) summit of the Collserola hills behind the city. With the haze caused by city traffic there is usually a fine view only of the skyline, but on rare occasions the view reaches across Barcelona to the

sea, the Balearic Islands, north to the Pyrenees and west to Montserrat.

An afternoon or evening out at these dizzy heights can be a family occasion, starting with hands-on fun at CosmoCaixa, Barcelona's science museum, before continuing up the hill to take in the Tibidabo amusement park.

TRAMVIA BLAU

Getting up the hill is part of the fun. Take the FGC train to **Avinguda Tibidabo** ❶ station, then cross Passeig de Sant Gervasi. Here, at the beginning of Avinguda del Tibidabo, is the stop for the old-fashioned, open-sided wooden **Tramvia Blau** (Blue Tram) that will take you to the funicular that goes up to Tibidabo every 30 minutes. The tram is part of the original Barcelona tram system and in 2011 celebrated 100 years in operation. The more frequent No. 195 bus, which leaves from the stop a few steps further on, also goes to the fun park.

Avinguda del Tibidabo
The ride up this grand avenue takes you past Modernista houses and villas, built for the city's elite intent on escaping the hassle of industrial Barcelona, and characterised by lavish turrets and tiles. The villa at No. 31 is now the smart **El Asador de Aranda**, see ⑪①.

COSMOCAIXA

Part way up the hill, en route to the funicular (about 15 minutes' walk or two stops on bus No. 60) is the science museum, **CosmoCaixa** ❷ (Carrer de Isaac Newton 26; tel: 93 212 60 50; www.obrasocial.lacaixi.es; Tue–Sun 10am–8pm; charge). Situated on the left just before the Ronda de Dalt highway, it is one of the most entertaining museums in the city.

There are numerous interactive exhibits, including energy and force machines, and computers to test reflexes, equilibrium, colour awareness and ability to lie. There are also microscopes and satellite pictures, even a submarine. Click and Flash, an area aimed at 3- to 6-year-olds, was created by designer Xavier Mariscal to give little ones their first taste of science, through stimulating interactive displays. The newest facility, the Planetarium, projects a stereoscopic 3D effect, using the latest technology to immerse viewers in the action.

When you have finished at the museum, continue up the hill towards the funicular, or return to the bus stop, if you can't face the walk.

Drinks with a View
Once across the Ronda de Dalt, the road winds through bosky estates pep-

Food and Drink 🍴

① EL ASADOR DE ARANDA
Avinguda del Tibidabo 31; tel: 93 417 01 15; www.asadordearanda.com; Mon–Sat 1–4pm, 9pm–midnight; €€€
The flagship of this high-quality chain of restaurants serves typically hearty Castilian food. The house speciality is lamb roasted in a clay oven.

Above from left:
toy museum;
Madonna depicted in
stained glass at the
Sagrat Cor; Viking
ride at Parc
d'Atraccions.

High Flyer
The red aeroplane
ride (Avion Tibiair) at
Tibidabo began in
1928.

pered with Modernist fantasies until it
reaches the funicular station at Plaça del
Doctor Andreu. Here, there is a choice
of places to stop for a drink with great
views over the city, including **La Venta**,
see ⑪②, and **Mirablau**, see ⑪③.

The Funicular

The Art Deco funicular, which opened
in 1901, runs to the top of Tibidabo,
taking seven minutes to ascend its
almost vertical track. Choose whether
to buy a single or return ticket (a return
is slightly cheaper than two singles).
If you fancy a 30-minute bus ride back
to Plaça de Catalunya from the top –
or a walk down – plump for a single.

Food and Drink 🍴

② LA VENTA
Plaça del Doctor Andreu s/n; tel: 93 212 64 55; www.restaurant
elaventa.com; Tue–Sun 1.30–3.30pm, 9–11.30pm; €€€
Stylish bar and restaurant offering Catalan dishes.

③ MIRABLAU
Plaça del Doctor Andreu 2; tel: 93 418 58 79;
www.mirablaubcn.com; Mon–Thur 11am–4.30am, Fri–Sun
11am–5.30am; €€€
Restaurant and cocktail lounge with a terrace and stunning
views. Used as a nightclub in the evening.

④ RESTAURANT LA MASIA
Plaça del Tibidabo 3–4; tel: 93 417 63 50; daily 10.30am–8pm;
€€
Sandwiches and snacks are served on the outdoor terrace of
Hotel La Masia.

⑤ GRAN HOTEL LA FLORIDA
Carretera de Vallvidrera al Tibidabo 83–93; tel: 93 259 30 00;
restaurant: Tue–Sat 7–11am, 1–3.30pm, 8.30–11pm, Mon
7–11am, 1–3.30pm only; €€€
Opened in 1925, this grand venue has now been revitalised.
You can eat at L'Orangerie, the lovely restaurant, or just drop in
for a drink at the bar.

PARC D'ATRACCIONS

The **Parc d'Atraccions ❸** (Plaça del
Tibidabo; tel: 93 211 79 42; www. tibi
dabo.cat; Aug Wed–Sun noon–11pm,
July Wed–Fri noon–9pm, Sat–Sun
noon–10pm, Mar–June Sat–Sun
noon–7pm, Sept–Oct noon–9pm,
Nov–Dec noon–6pm; charge; all-in
tickets permit unlimited access to the
rides. Dating back to 1901, this amusement park is one of the oldest in the
world. With over 25 rides, street shows,
theatre and other entertainment for all
ages, the park can take a good few hours
to explore properly. Many of the old
favourites remain but there is now a new
generation of theme-park rides. The
majority are still fairly tame but La
Muntanya Russa, a head-spinning
rollercoaster, and Avion Tibiair, a red
plane, a replica of the first to fly between

Madrid and Barcelona, that swoops off the side of the hill, are both likely to give you an adrenalin rush. Check out the Sky Walk, an area with the best views of Barcelona. There is also a **Museu de Automàts**, with mechanical toys from the first half of the 20th century.

THE SAGRAT COR

There is more to Tibidabo than the funfair – there are restaurants with panoramic views, including **La Masia** and the **Gran Hotel La Florida**, see ⑪④ and ⑪⑤, and pleasant paths to walk. Many people come here to visit the **Sagrat Cor** (Plaça del Tibidabo tel: 93 417 56 96; www.templotibidabo. org; daily 10.30am–3pm, 4–7pm; charge), the Sacred Heart church, a bulky 20th-century architectural confection on the site of a chapel used by the hermit Joan Bosco, in the 19th century. There is a lift in the tower up to the top from where there are marvellous views of the city. The original chapel can be seen behind the main church.

TORRE DE COLLSEROLA

At this point you may wish to return to the city, but if you are up for an even more spectacular view, go down the road behind the Hotel La Masia to the **Torre de Collserola** ❹ (tel: 93 406 93 54; www.torrecollserola.com; same hours as Parc d'Atraccions; charge), which you will undoubtedly have seen ever since your arrival on Tibidabo. You can take the lift to the glassed-in observation platform on the

10th floor of the 288m (945ft) communications tower. Designed by British architect Norman Foster for the 1992 Olympics, it is sometimes known as **Torre Foster**.

If you wanted to return a different way you could walk on for another 20 minutes or so, to reach the Modernista funicular station of **Vallvidrera Superior**. The funicular takes you down to the FGC station at **Peu del Funicular**, from where it is only a 15-minute train ride back to Plaça de Catalunya.

Model Pilots
Members of the Club Vellers Collserola turn out on the hills most evenings in summer to fly their model planes, and they organise competitions throughout the year. The models have wingspans of up to 5m (15ft).

The Collserola Hills

The Collserola park, on the other side of the hill from the funfair, is a great place for walks, cycling or picnics. A mere 13-minute train ride from Plaça de Catalunya through a tunnel takes you to Baixador de Vallvidrera. Here you step out into another world, with the pine-scented air hitting you as soon as the doors open. Walk up the landscaped path to the Centre d'Informació del Parc de Collserola (tel: 93 280 35 52; www.parcnaturalcollserola.cat; 9.30am–3pm), a helpful base, with maps, advice, an exhibition on wildlife, and a bar/restaurant. Close by is the atmospheric Villa Joana (tel: 93 204 11 85; Sat–Sun 10am–2pm; free), where the much-loved poet Jacinct Verdaguer lived until his death in 1902.

Footpaths lead into the woods with *fonts* (natural springs) and picnic spots. To explore further, take the funicular from Peu del Funicular to Vallvidrera and get off halfway up at Carretera de les Aigües, a track that is popular with joggers, cyclists, ramblers and model-plane makers.

SITGES

Just 40km (25 miles) south of Barcelona and generally sunnier, the elegant seaside town of Sitges has a rich artistic heritage, having long attracted painters, writers and other creative people. Since the 1960s, it has been the focal point of the gay scene on this stretch of coastal northeastern Spain.

Above: beach slides; prawns fresh from the sea.

American Route
The Sitges tourist office (Plaça Eduard Maristany 2; tel: 93 894 42 51; www.sitges tur.cat; Mon–Fri 10am–2pm, 4–6.30pm, Sat 10am–3pm, 4–7pm, Sun 10am–2pm) offers an 'Americanos Route' tour that takes in the villas and mansions built by Sitges' sons and daughters who returned from their prosperous ventures in the Americas.

> **DISTANCE** 40km (25 miles) one way
> **TIME** A full day
> **START** Sitges train station
> **END** Cementiri de Sant Sebastià
> **POINTS TO NOTE**
> Regular trains to Sitges run from Passeig de Gràcia or Sants stations (line C2; around 40 minutes). By car, the C32 motorway has been blasted through the Garraf mountains to alleviate the congested motorway. Don't forget your swimming costume.

Food and Drink

① REVES
Carrer de Sant Francesc 35; tel: 93 894 76 25; Tue–Sat 1.30–4.30pm, 8.30–11.30pm; €€
Attractive restaurant/tapas bar near the station. Tasty menu featuring the local speciality *xató de sitges* (salad with anchovies, tuna and salt cod).

② EL CELLER VELL
Carrer Sant Bonaventura 21; tel: 93 811 19 61; www.elcellervell.com; Fri–Tue 1–3.30pm, 8.15–11pm, Thur 8.15–11pm; €€
This old cellar with rustic decor serves good traditional Catalan cooking: grilled meats and fish and specials such as rabbit with artichokes. Good value set meals too.

The best known of the coastal resorts within easy reach of Barcelona, Sitges is an attractive, cosmopolitan place with excellent shops, great restaurants and a buzzing gay scene.

The Making of a Resort
A former wine town that had trade links with America, Sitges prospered in the 19th century, when so-called *americanos*, local people who had found fortune abroad, came home to retire in mansions and build summer houses.

The Luminist School of Sitges, comprising artists such as Joan Roig i Soler and Arcadi Mas i Fontdevila, were attracted by the superior quality of light in this seaside town in the second half of the 19th century. However, when *fin-de-siècle* Modernista artist and writer Santiago Rusiñol (1861–1931) bought a home here in 1891, Sitges was dubbed 'the Mecca of Modernisme' by the Barcelona press, and Rusiñol was credited with having discovered the place.

The resort's popularity with the bohemian crowd continued: Spanish poet and playwright Federico García Lorca (1899–1936) stayed here, as did the French composer Erik Satie (1866–1925) and the English writer G.K. Chesterton (1874–1936).

In the late 1950s and early 1960s Sitges responded to the flood of tourists to the coast with pubs, bars and a few hotels; local people rented out rooms in summer, and a few entrepreneurs built modest apartment blocks. It was at this point that the town began to attract the gay community.

TOWARDS THE OLD TOWN

As you exit from **Sitges station ❶** you will pass the renovated municipal **Mercat** (Mon–Sat 8.30am–2pm, also Tue, Thur, Fri 5.30–8.30pm). If you want to eat while you are in the vicinity of the station, two recommendations for food are **Reves**, see ⑪①, and **El Celler Vell**, see ⑪②.

From the station, all roads seem to lead down to the sea. The first three cross Carrer de Sant Gaudenci and lead to **Plaça Cap de La Vila ❷**, the heart of the pedestrianised shopping area, with numerous cafés and bars spilling on to the street.

Left of here, on Carrer d'Angel Vidal, is the **Pati Blau**, a recreation of a painting of a blue courtyard by Rusiñol. Straight ahead is Carrer Major, which takes you down to the old town.

MUSEU ROMÀNTIC

At this point, however, our recommendation is a detour to the right down Carrer de Parallades, a busy shopping street, then first right into Carrer de Sant Gaudenci for the **Museu Romàntic ❸** (Casa Llopis, Carrer de Sant Gaudenci 1; tel: 93 894 29 69; summer Tue–Sat 9.30am–2pm, 4–7pm, Sun

Above from far left: view of the rooftops of Sitges; the town's busy beach, Platja d'Or.

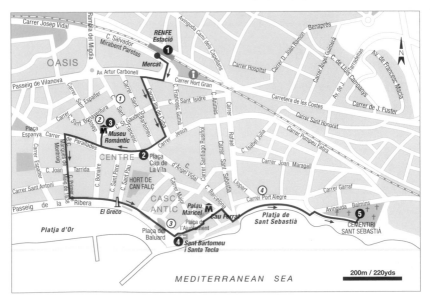

Above from left: tiled frieze; view of the town from the beach.

10am–3pm, winter Tue–Sat 9.30am–2pm, 3.30–6.30pm, Sun 10am–3pm; guided tours on the hour also include entrance to the town's other main museums, with the same opening times; charge). This house, built in 1793 by the cultured Llopis family, was given in its entirety to the town as a museum of family life. On the top floor is a large collection of antique dolls amassed by local children's writer Lola Anglada (1893–1984).

CARRER DEL PECAT

Xató
Fried fish and squid dishes are popular in seaside Sitges, but a local speciality is *xató*, a salad of escarole (a variety of endive), tuna, dried cod and anchovies, with a dressing that may include nuts and peppers.

Continue down Carrer de Parallades to Carrer del Marqués de Montroig and turn left into Carrer Primer de Maig de 1838 – the date, 1 May, commemorates an attack on the liberal town by reactionary Carlists. This is the main pedestrian avenue running down to the sea, lined with bars and sun-seekers at café tables, and popularly known as the Street of Sin, **Carrer del Pecat**.

This is the focal point for some of the largest events in Sitges' busy festive calendar. At Corpus Christi (in June), the street is covered in a carpet of flowers, while during the pre-Lent carnival parade, there is an elaborate show of costume and design here. The Shrove Tuesday evening parade is probably the town's most outrageous spectacle, with the glamour hitting top notes at the transvestite festival, complete with glitzy costumes.

THE BEACH

At the bottom of the street is the palm-fringed promenade Passeig de la Ribera, which is lined by the gently curving **Platja d'Or**, a golden strand some 5km (3 miles) long. If you are hungry at this point and would like an up-market lunch, continue to the left, towards the end of the beach promenade for **Fragata**, see ⑪③.

PALAU MARICEL

The beach ends just beyond the monument to the painter El Greco on the rocky promontory that is dominated by the 17th-century church of **Sant Bartomeu i Santa Tecla ④**.

Just behind the church, in Carrer Fonollar, are some magnificent white mansions and, on the left at Nos 2–6, the **Palau Maricel** (tel: 93 894 03 64; tours as part of a summer programme; call for details), with a lovely blue-tiled roof terrace. The palace was built in 1910 by the American philanthropist Charles Deering (1852–1927) to house

Food and Drink 🍴

③ FRAGATA
Passeig de la Ribera 1; tel: 93 894 10 86; www.restaurante fragata.com; daily 1.30–4.30pm, 8.30–11.30pm; €€€€
Situated among a cluster of restaurants at the end of the promenade near the church of Sant Bartolomeu i Santa Tecla, this unfussy restaurant serves top-notch seafood specialities, and meat dishes, too.

④ COSTA DORADO
Carrer Port Alegre 27; tel: 93 894 35 43; www.restaurantecostadorada.com; Fri–Wed 1–4.30pm, 8–11pm (closed Wed evening in winter); €€€
On a quieter stretch of the seafront, this bright, airy restaurant has been in the same family since 1968. There is an emphasis on fresh seafood, and it's a good place to try *xató (see above)*.

his art collection (sadly now dispersed). Concerts are sometimes held here.

Deering also purchased the building opposite, a former hospital dating from the 14th century, and connected it to his own palace by an overhead passageway. The hospital now houses the **Museu Maricel** (Carrer Fonollar; tel: 93 894 03 64; closed for renovation, due to reopen summer 2013; check for details of opening times; charge), with a fine collection of Gothic paintings and furniture and a room decorated by Josep Luís Sert. This is also the home of the town's main art collection, with works by the Romantics, Luminists and Modernistas who were associated with Sitges; a portrait of Deering by Ramón Casas is among them.

SANTIAGO RUSIÑOL

The neighbouring building is home to the **Museu Cau Ferrat** (Carrer Fonollar; tel: 93 894 03 64; www.mnac. es; closed for renovation, due to reopen end 2012; check for details of opening times; charge), erstwhile home of the painter Santiago Rusiñol and now the showcase for his collection, including two El Grecos (bought in Paris, they were carried through the town, with a statue of the artist, in a mock Holy Week procession), five small Picassos and works by Casas.

Like many artists of his generation, Rusiñol was funded by his family, which had grown rich thanks to Barcelona's industrial revolution. Rusiñol travelled frequently to Paris, forging important links for local artists. He purchased fishermen's cottages in Sitges, which he converted into a mansion to house his collection of ironwork, sculptures and paintings and to use as a studio. Between 1892 and 1899 he also organised the Festes Modernistes, a music and drama festival.

SANT SEBASTIÀ BEACH

North of these imposing buildings is **Platja de Sant Sebastià**. Quieter than the main beach, it offers good restaurants, including **Costa Dorada**, see ⑪④, and pavement cafés.

If it is not too hot, or if you tire of the beach, an option is to head up the scrubby paths on the far side of Platja de Sant Sebastià towards the atmospheric **Cementiri de Sant Sebastià** ❺ (Avinguda Balmins; tel: 93 706 57 28; summer Mon–Sat 9am–1pm, 3–6pm, Sun 9am–1pm, winter Mon–Sat 8am–1pm, 3–5pm, Sun 9am–1pm; 1 Nov 8am–6pm; free), the town's cemetery.

A Way of Life
Una manera de ser meaning 'A way of life' or just 'a way of being' is the official Sitges slogan. It is one appreciated by the gay community, and is taken up on the website www. gaysitges.com, which gives up-to-date news about the town.

Below: detail of Santiago Rusiñol's *Morphine* (1894).

WINE TOUR

Catalonia is a major wine-producing region, known for its cava. A tour of the Penedès region gives you a chance to see some lovely countryside as well as tasting various delicious wines.

Seaside Drive
If you have a hire car, a trip through the Penedès vineyards could be combined with a visit to Sitges (*see pp.90–3*). If not, there are travel agencies and tour operators that organise wine and gastronomy tours from Barcelona. The most comprehensive information on visits to some 300 wine and cava producers can be found at the Vilafranca Tourist Office (Carrer Cort 14; tel: 93 818 12 54; www.turisme vilafranca.com).

DISTANCE 55km (35 miles)

TIME A full day

START Sant Sadurní d'Anoia

END Vilafranca

POINTS TO NOTE

Take the train from Barcelona Sants or Plaça de Catalunya (Mon–Sat every 30 mins 5.20am–11pm, Sun and hols every hour; journey time 45 mins). To continue by train to Vilafranca, just 10–15 mins further, take the same line. By car, take the A2/A7 motorway from Barcelona (direction Tarragona). Many wineries close in August, and the wine museum is closed on Monday.

Food and Drink

① **CAL TON**

Carrer de Casal 8; Vilafranca del Penedès; tel: 93 890 37 41; www.restaurantcalton.com; Tue and Sun 1–4pm, Wed–Sat 1–4pm, 8.30–10.30pm; €€€
Chef Toni Mata has a reputation for innovative modern Catalan cooking using the best of the local ingredients.

② **CASA JOAN**

Plaça de l'Estació 8; Vilafranca del Penedès; tel: 93 890 21 71; Mon–Sat 1–4pm; €€
Right by the station. High-quality Catalan dishes and delicious desserts.

Catalonia's most significant contribution to the world of wine is cava, an inexpensive, earthy, non-acidic sparkling drink produced in the same way as Champagne, but by law forbidden the French *appellation*. Around 90 percent of the country's output comes from the Penedès region, south of Barcelona, in vineyards around the town of Sant Sadurní d'Anoia. Catalonia's main wine town is nearby Vilafranca del Penedès.

Visiting both Sant Sadurní and Vilafranca will give you a flavour not just of the product but of the countryside. For details of how to get to Sant Sadurní, see the grey box left.

SANT SADURNÍ D'ANOIA

Freixenet

Beside the station at **Sant Sadurní d'Anoia** ❶ is **Freixenet** (Carrer de Joan Sala 2; tel: 93 891 70 00; www. freixenet.es; Mon–Sat 10am–6pm, Sun 10am–2.30pm (seasonal variations); charge), one of the largest producers in the region. There are regular 90-minute tours of the cellars with tastings, plus a trip in a miniature train and opportunities to buy afterwards.

Codorníu

Even more impressive is the original home of cava, **Codorníu** (Avinguda de

Jaume Codorníu; tel: 93 891 33 42; www.codorniu.com; pre-arranged tours only; charge), about 20 minutes' walk (signposted) from the station. Josep Raventós, of the Codorníu family dynasty, popped the first cava cork here in 1872, and his son Manuel added the huge Modernista cellars, designed by Puig i Cadafalch, from 1902–15. The cellars are now a national monument. A tour of Codorníu includes an explanation of the wine-making business, a tour of the museum at the winery and a train ride through part of the five storeys of cellars that cover some 26km (16 miles).

VILAFRANCA

Opportunities for lunch in a small country town such as Sant Sadurní are fairly limited, so at this point we recommend continuing to **Vilafranca del Penedès ②**, slightly further down the railway line (also on the A7). There are some excellent restaurants here, including the up-market **Cal Ton**, see ⑪① (note the plaque that indicates that it is on the **Ruta del Vi i del Cava**,

the Route of Wine and Cava). Conveniently situated right next to the station is traditional **Casa Joan**, also known for good local wines, see ⑪②.

Torres

All the bars bear the motto *Hi ha Cava a copes* (There is cava by the glass here), but Vilafranca is actually the centre for still-wine production. The old bodega of the great **Torres** family is at Carrer de Comercio 22, beside the station. You can also visit their state-of-the-art winery at **Pacs** (tel: 93 817 74 87; www.torres.es; Mon–Sat 9.15am–4.45pm, Sun 9.15am–1pm; charge), just outside the town.

Museu del Vi

Spain's best wine museum, the **Museu del Vi** (Plaça de Jaume I 1; tel: 93 890 05 32; Tue–Sat June–Aug 10am–7pm, Sept–May 10am–2pm, 4–7pm, Sun 10am–2pm all year; charge includes tasting) occupies a former royal palace in Plaça de Jaume I, opposite the basilica of Santa Maria. The museum showcases wine-making implements, and a bar displays the region's wine.

Above from far left: stained-glass window at the Museu del Vi in Vilafranca; cellars at Freixenet.

Above: some of the different types of cava produced at Freixenet.

Human Pyramids Wall tiles in the Plaça de la Villa in Vilafranca celebrate the *castellers*. These human towers are attempted at the end of August as teams, physically supported by the crowds, compete for height, balance and skill.

DALÍ TOUR

The Surrealist artist Salvador Dalí was born and lived in the Empordà region, where his museum, home and the castle he gave to his wife Gala – the 'Dalí Triangle' – are worthy legacies of his eccentricity and talent.

Gala

In 1929 Dalí met Russian-born Elena Ivanovna Diakonova (1894–1982), and nicknamed her Gala. She had previously been married to the poet Paul Eluard, with whom she had a daughter, and had also had a relation-ship with Max Ernst. She and Dalí married in 1958.

DISTANCE 80km (50 miles)

TIME At least a full day

START Figueres

END Port Lligat or Púbol

POINTS TO NOTE

This route includes three main sights: the Teatre-Museu Dalí in Figueres; Dalí's house in Port Lligat; and the Castell Gala-Dalí at Púbol. The first is accessible by train from Barcelona; the second by bus, but to visit all three sights, you will need to hire a car.

FIGUERES

Salvador Dalí was born in 1904 in the pleasant market town of **Figueres ❶** some 24km (15 miles) from the French border. Here he founded a permanent home for his work at **Teatre-Museu Dalí** (Plaça Gala-Salvador Dalí 5; tel: 972 67 75 00; www.salvadordali. org/museus/figueres; July–Sept daily 9am–8pm, Mar–June and Oct 9.30am–6pm, Nov–Feb 10.30am–6pm; charge). Opened in 1974, the museum was built on the site of a the-atre that was burned down at the end of the Civil War. The adjacent Torre Galatea (named after his wife, Gala), added in 1981, is where Dalí died in 1989. He is buried in the crypt in the museum's lower level.

The Collection

Among the extraordinary works here are the *Poetry of America, or Cosmic Athletes*, painted in 1943, a portrait of Gala as Leda (the swan), and the huge ceiling fresco dominating the Wind Palace Room on the first floor. In the garden, the *Rainy Cadillac* sculpture is a crowd puller. In the adjoining annexe you can see the dazzling exhi-bition of Dalí's jewels.

A good place to eat in Figueres is the **Hotel Empordà**, see ⑪①.

PORT LLIGAT

From Figueres it is around 40km (25 miles) east on the C260 and GI614 to the seaside town of **Cadaqués**.

Casa-Museu Dalí

Located just over the hill, in the next cove, is **Port Lligat ❷** and the seafront **Casa-Museu Dalí** (Port Lligat; tel: 972 25 10 15; www.salvador-dali. org/museus/portlligat; mid-Feb–mid-June and mid-Sept–Dec Tue–Sun 10.30am–6pm, mid-June–mid-Sept daily 9.30am–9pm; booking essential; charge). Dalí and Gala lived for many years in this gorgeous house, actually a collection of fishermen's cottages.

Set in a garden of gnarled olive trees (where a restored workshop features a new exhibition), the house offers insight into the Dalís' domestic life. Huge windows frame views of the fishermen's cove and the Mediterranean, and in the Yellow Room a mirror is angled so Dalí could see the light of the rising sun while in bed in the open-plan adjoining room.

Gala's touch is visible in many areas, particularly in the Room of the Cupboards, where she covered cupboard doors with photographs and magazine covers, and in the 'everlasting flowers' with which she festooned the windows.

The swimming pool area is an example of Dalían kitsch: modelled on a pool at the Moorish Alhambra in Granada, it is embellished with a statue of Diana the Huntress, models of Michelin men and Pirelli tyres.

If it is time for lunch, **Hotel Port Lligat**, see ⑪②, is just across the road.

PÚBOL

To continue the tour (only possible if you are travelling by car, as there are poor public transport connections between Port Lligat and Púbol), head back in the direction of Figueres until you see signs for the C31 south to Girona. Continue on this road until you hit the C252, towards Púbol.

Castell Gala-Dalí

The highlight in Púbol is the **Castell Gala-Dalí ❸** (Plaça Gala-Dalí; tel: 972 48 86 55; www.salvador-dali.org/ museus/pubol; mid-June–mid Sept daily 10am–8pm, mid-Mar–mid-June, mid-Sept–Oct Tue–Sun 10.30am–6pm, Nov–Dec Tue–Sat 10am–5pm; charge). Dalí restored this magnificent Gothic-Renaissance castle and presented it to Gala in 1970, promising only to enter it at her invitation. He painted frescoes in the interior and built the crypt where Gala is buried. On the day of her death in 1982 he moved into it himself and stayed, becoming increasingly frail, until a fire two years later obliged him to move to Torre Galatea.

Above from far left: exterior of the Teatre-Museu Dalí in Figueres; spectacular ceiling fresco at the Teatre-Museu Dalí.

Above: the Teatre-Museu, Figueres; the inimitable Salvador Dalí; crowds outside the museum.

Food and Drink

① HOTEL EMPORDÀ
Avenida Salvador Dalí i Domènech 170; Figueres; tel: 972 50 05 62; www.hotelemporada.com; daily 7.30–11am, 12.45–3.45pm, 8.30–10.45pm; €€€
The late chef Josep Mercadé was one of the first to reinvent Catalan dishes, and his approach is still strongly evident here.

② HOTEL PORT LLIGAT
Port Lligat; tel: 972 25 81 62; www.port-lligat.net/hotel; Apr–Sept daily 1.30–3pm, 8.30–10pm; €€
This pleasant little café is in a lovely spot opposite Dalí's house.

DIRECTORY

A user-friendly alphabetical listing of practical information, plus hand-picked hotels and restaurants, clearly organised by area, to suit all budgets and tastes, together with some nightlife recommendations.

A

ADMISSION CHARGES

Most museums have an entry charge, with the usual reductions for children, students and the over-65s. The Articket (€30) allows entry to Barcelona's seven main museums for three months (www.articketbcn.org). The Arqueoticket (€14) provides entry to five museums with archaeological collections and is valid for a year.

C

CHILDREN

Children under five go free on public transport but pay full price from five upwards. However, child fares do apply on the Tourist Bus and there are Tourist Cards for children aged 4–13. In museums the age at which children go free, or pay a reduced price, varies. Some larger hotels have childcare services. For babysitters, try Tender Loving Canguros (www.tlcanguros.com).

CLIMATE

Barcelona's mild Mediterranean climate assures sunshine most of the year and freezing temperatures are rare, even in winter. Spring and autumn are the most agreeable seasons. Midsummer can be hot and humid; at times a thick mist hangs over the city. Average temperatures in winter are 10°C (54°F), and 25°C (75°F) in summer. Nov and Feb–Mar are the wettest months.

Age Restrictions
The legal age for buying and consuming tobacco and alcohol is 18. You must be 21 to hire a car.

CLOTHING

Barcelonans are generally stylish, and dress codes are informal but elegant. Men are expected to wear jackets in the more up-market restaurants. Jeans are fine for informal spots, but you will not see many local people eating out in shorts and trainers, except at beachside cafés. From November to April you will need a warm jacket or sweater and raincoat. The rest of the year, light summer clothing is in order, with a hat or umbrella in case of showers.

CRIME AND SAFETY

Be on your guard against pickpockets and bag snatchers (be wary of people offering 'assistance' or becoming suddenly interested in you), especially in the Rambla and Old Town, and at major tourist sights. Try to avoid deserted alleyways. Do not leave luggage unattended; do not carry more money than you need for daily expenses; use the hotel safe for larger sums and valuables; photocopy personal documents and leave the originals in your hotel; wear cameras strapped across your body; do not leave valuables on view in a car. The blue-clad, mobile anti-crime squads are out in force on the Rambla and principal thoroughfares. Should you be a crime victim, make a report *(denuncia)* at the nearest police station *(comisaría)* – vital for insurance claims. The main one in the Old Town is at Nou de la Rambla, 76–78, or call the Mossos d'Esquadra (088 or 112). From summer 2012 you can report theft at most city hotels.

CUSTOMS

Free exchange of non-duty-free items for personal use is permitted between Spain and other EU countries (300 cigarettes, limited amounts of alcohol and perfume). Visitors may bring up to €6,000 into or out of Spain without a declaration. If you intend to bring in and take out larger sums, declare this on arrival and departure.

D

DISABLED TRAVELLERS

The city has many hotels with facilities (see www.barcelona-access.com, or check with the tourist office). Many museums and historic buildings are wheelchair-accessible. The beaches have suitable access, and there are many adapted public toilets. Some bus and metro lines have facilities for disabled travellers (see www.tmb.net). For adapted taxi information, call tel: 93 223 5151.

For further information contact the Institut Municipal de Persones amb Discapacitat (Carrer de València 344, 08013 Barcelona; tel: 93 413 27 75; www.bcn.cat/imd; Mon–Fri 9am–2pm).

E

ELECTRICITY

The standard is 220 volts, but some hotels have 110–120 in the bathrooms as a safety precaution. Check before plugging in any of your appliances.

Power sockets take round, two-pin plugs, so British visitors will need an international adapter. US visitors will also need a transformer, unless they have dual-voltage travel appliances.

EMBASSIES AND CONSULATES

Most Western European countries have consulates in Barcelona. All the embassies are in Madrid.

Canada: Plaça de Catalunya 9; tel: 93 270 36 14.

Ireland: Gran Vía Carles III 94; tel: 93 491 50 21.

UK: Avinguda Diagonal 477, 13º; tel. 90 210 93 56.

US: Passeig de la Reina Elisenda 23; tel: 93 280 22 27.

EMERGENCIES

General emergencies: 112
Mossos d'Esquadra (Autonomous Catalan Police): 088
Municipal (city) police: 092
Fire: 080

G

GAY AND LESBIAN TRAVELLERS

Barcelona has an active gay community and scores of clubs and nightlife options. Conservative Catholic beliefs still predominate in some sectors, so gay visitors may wish to be discreet. The gay and lesbian hotline is 900 601

Above from far left: view from Park Güell; Mercat de Santa Caterina.

Etiquette
Barcelona is a fairly relaxed, informal city, yet it is always worth paying attention to local etiquette. It is respectful to cover up when visiting churches. Shaking hands is a common form of greeting, and physical contact, such as back patting, is a friendly gesture. Air kissing, touching right cheeks first, then the left, comes later. Even when addressing a stranger, the familiar *tú* is used more often than the formal *vosotros*.

601. The free magazine *Nois* has information and listings of clubs, restaurants and other entertainment options. Casal Lambda is a gay cultural centre (Carrer de Verdaguer i Callis 10; tel: 93 319 55 50; email: infor@lambaweb.org; open from 5pm).

The nearby town of Sitges, just half an hour south of the city on the coast, is a real magnet for gay people, particularly in summer, and is well worth a visit *(see p.90)*.

GOVERNMENT

Spain is a constitutional monarchy headed by King Juan Carlos I. The parliament *(Cortes)* has a Congress of Deputies (Lower House) with 350 members elected by proportional representation every four years. Catalonia is one of 17 autonomous regions, which elect a total of 49 members to the Senate. Catalonia is governed by the Generalitat in Plaça de Sant Jaume opposite the Ajuntament (town hall), where the mayor and the city council preside.

H

HEALTH

Standards of hygiene are high, and medical care is generally excellent; most doctors speak sufficient English.

It is wise to ease yourself into the climate and food gently. In summer, is it advisable to wear a hat and suncream during the day. You should also avoid any tired-looking tapas, particularly those that are mayonnaise-based, during the hotter months, as these could be a possible source of infection. The water is safe to drink, but can have a strong taste; bottled water is inexpensive.

EU citizens with corresponding health insurance facilities are entitled to medical and hospital treatment under the Spanish social security system – you need a **European Health Insurance Card**, obtainable from post offices or online. However, it is always advisable to take out private medical insurance.

In an emergency, go to the *Urgencias* department of a main hospital:
Hospital de la Santa Creu i Sant Pau: Carrer de Sant Antoni Maria Claret 167; tel: 93 291 90 00 (behind the Sagrada Família).
Hospital Clinic i Provincial: Carrer de Casanova 143; tel: 93 227 54 00.
Hospital de Sant Joan de Déu: Passeig Sant Joan de Déu 2; tel: 93 253 21 00.

For an ambulance, go to an *ambulatorio* (medical centre) or call 061.

Pharmacies *(farmàcia)* operate as a first line of defence, as pharmacists can prescribe drugs and are usually adept at making on-the-spot diagnoses. There is always one in each district that stays open all night and on public holidays.

HOLIDAYS

Many bars, restaurants and museums close in the afternoon and evening on public holidays and Sundays. August is the annual holiday month, and many businesses, including restaurants, may close down for three or four weeks.

1 Jan: *Año Nuevo* (New Year's Day)

6 Jan: *Epifanía* (Epiphany)

1 May: *Fiesta de Trabajo* (Labour Day)

24 June: *San Juan* (St John's Day)

15 Aug: *Asunción* (Assumption)

11 Sept: *La Diada*
(Catalan National Day)

24 Sept: *La Mercè* (Day of Mercedes,
Barcelona's patron saint)

1 Nov: *Todos los Santos*
(All Saints' Day)

6 Dec: *Día de la Constitución*
(Constitution Day)

8 Dec: *Inmaculada Concepció*
(Immaculate Conception)

25–26 Dec: *Navidad* (Christmas)

Movable Feasts:

Feb/Mar: *Mardi Gras* (Shrove
Tuesday/Carnival)

Late Mar/Apr: *Viernes Santo*
(Good Friday)

Late Mar/Apr: *Lunes de Pascua*
(Easter Monday)

Early to mid-June: *Corpus Christi*
(Corpus Christi)

I

INTERNET

There are numerous places where internet access is cheap and easy but be aware that internet cafés are notorious for going out of business. Try easyInternet Café (La Rambla 31; daily 8am–2.30am); Ciber Virreina (Plaça de la Virreina; Mon–Fri 9am–1am, Sat–Sun 9am–10pm); inetcorner (Carrer de Sardenya 306; Mon–Sat 10am–10pm, Sun noon–8pm).

L

LANGUAGE

English is understood by a large number people working in the tourist industry. Both Catalan *(català)* and Castilian Spanish *(castellano)* are official languages in Catalonia; you can assume that everyone in Barcelona who speaks Catalan can also speak Spanish, even if they prefer not to, but because many residents come to the city from other parts of the country, they will not all speak Catalan.

Street signs are in Catalan, but labels in museums and items on menus are usually in both languages. Learning some Catalan will be appreciated *(see back cover of pull-out map for a few helpful phrases)*, but Spanish (Castilian) will certainly get you by.

LEFT LUGGAGE

Left-luggage lockers *(consigna)* are available in the main railway stations (Sants and Estació de França), at Barcelona Nord bus station, at the sea terminal on Moll de Sant Bertran and at El Prat airport. Or try Locker Barcelona (Carrer Estruc 36; www.lockerbarcelona.com) in the city centre just off Plaça de Catalunya.

LOST PROPERTY

There is a lost property office at Plaça de Carles Pi i Sunyer 8, close to Plaça de Catalunya; Mon–Fri 9am–2pm; tel: 93 413 2031.

Dentists
The cost of dental care in Spain for non-Spaniards is not covered by any of the reciprocal agreements between countries, so make sure that your travel insurance covers treatment. In the case of an emergency, visit the Clínica Dental Barcelona (Passeig de Gràcia 97; tel: 93 487 83 29; emergency service daily 9am–midnight). English-speaking dentists available.

M

MEDIA

Newspapers: A large number of European newspapers and the Paris-based *International Herald Tribune* are sold on the day of publication at newsstands on La Rambla and the Passeig de Gràcia, as well as in Fnac on Plaça de Catalunya. Principal European and American magazines are also widely available in the city.

Metropolitan, Barcelona's monthly magazine in English, is free and has useful listings. For Spanish speakers, the handy *Guía del Ocio* lists bars, restaurants, and cinema, theatre and concert performances.

Television: The principal Spanish channels are TVE1 and TVE2 (state-owned), and TV3 and TV33, the autonomous Catalan channels. The local channel is BTV. Commercial channels include Antena 3 (general programming), Telecino and Canal Plus (mainly films, for subscribers only).

MONEY

Currency: The monetary unit of Spain is the euro (abbreviated to €). Notes are issued in denominations of 5, 10, 20, 50, 100, 200 and 500 euros. Coins in circulation are 1, 2, 5, 10, 20 and 50 centimos and 1 and 2 euros.

Currency Exchange: Banks and *cajas/caixes* (savings banks) are usually the best places to exchange currency, as they offer the most competitive rates with no commission. *Casas de cambio* (displaying a *cambio* sign) are convenient in that they open outside banking hours. Those advertising 'no commission' have lower exchange rates so you will in effect pay a hefty commission. Banks and exchange offices pay slightly more for traveller's cheques than for cash. Always take your passport when you go to change money.

Credit Cards: These are widely recognised, though smaller businesses tend to prefer cash. Photo identification is usually requested when paying with a card.

Cash Machines: These are ubiquitous. With displays in several languages, they will dispense money against your debit or credit card in just the same way that they do at home, using the same PIN.

Traveller's Cheques: Hotels, shops, restaurants and travel agencies all cash traveller's cheques, but banks generally give a better rate – you will always need your passport. Cash small amounts at a time, and keep the individual numbers of your cheques separately so they can be replaced quickly if they are lost or stolen.

O

OPENING TIMES

Banks: These generally open Mon–Fri 8.30am–2pm, and also Sat 8.30am–1pm in winter.

Maps
These are freely distributed by the tourist offices, and often left out for visitors in hotel rooms. There are also useful local wall maps at all metro stations.

Businesses: These open Mon–Fri 8 or 9am–2pm and 4–6 or 7pm. In summer, many office workers do *horas intensivas* (intensive hours) from 8am–3pm, to enable them to go home earlier.

Museums: Most are open Tue–Sat 10am–8pm, and Sun 10am–2.30pm. The majority close on Monday, but there are exceptions.

Restaurants: Some close one day a week, normally Monday or Sunday.

Shops: The big department and chain stores remain open throughout the day, from 10am–9.30pm, while traditional shops close for lunch in the early afternoon. Usual hours are Mon–Sat 10am–2pm and 4–8.30pm.

P

POLICE

The municipal and autonomous Catalan police are efficient and courteous – and generally very responsive to issues involving foreign tourists. In Barcelona, dial 092 for municipal (city) police and 088 for the autonomous Catalan police. The main police station in the Old Town is at Nou de la Rambla 76–8.

POST

The Central Post Office *(correus)* is in Plaça d'Antoni López, at the bottom of Via Laietana, in the vicinity of the port area (tel: 93 318 30 48; Mon–Fri 8.30am–9.30pm, Sat 8.30am–2pm).

Stamps can be purchased at the post office or at a tobacconists – look for the brown and yellow sign that reads '*Tabacs*'. Rates are divided into four areas of the world, just like telephone calls: the EU, rest of Europe, the US and Canada, and the rest of the world. Allow about one week for delivery to North America, and 4–5 days to the UK. To speed things up, send a letter *urgente* (express) or *certificado* (registered).

R

RELIGION

Roman Catholicism is the religion of Catalonia (and all of Spain) and Mass is said regularly in the churches of Barcelona. There are churches of most major faiths; the tourist information at Plaça de Catalunya has details on religious services, and those in foreign languages. Major ones include:
Anglican: St George's Church; Carrer Horaci 38, off Carrer de Sant Joan de la Salle 41; tel: 93 417 88 67.
Judaism: Synagogue: Carrer de l'Avenir 24; tel: 93 209 31 47.
Islam: Centro Islàmico; Avinguda Meridiana 326; tel: 93 351 49 01.

S

SPORT

Bicycles: Barcelona embraces the bike culture and in 2011 was the first city in Spain to install special traffic lights for

Above from far left: a nun in El Born; there are numerous shopping opportunities in Barcelona.

Smoking
In 2011 Spain introduced even more stringent smoking laws that are now among the strictest in Europe. Lighting up is banned in all public places, including bars and restaurants, on public transport, in offices, shops, schools, hospitals and theatres.

cyclists. Cycle lanes in the centre are well marked, and the traffic-free port, marinas and beach front are also great for cycling. Bikes can be rented at several outlets, such as Budget Bikes (Plaça de la Llana 3; tel: 93 304 18 85) and from Biciclot (Passeig Marítim de la Barceloneta 33; tel: 93 221 97 78), from where there is easy access to the Parc de la Ciutadella and the waterfront (tandems and child seats available).

Golf: There are many golf courses all over Catalonia: for a full list, see the tourist pages of www.gencat.cat. Weekend fees are usually double the weekday fee. Three courses close to Barcelona are: Real Club de El Prat (tel: 93 728 02 10), Sant Cugat (tel: 93 674 39 08) and Sitges Terramar (tel: 93 894 05 80).

Tennis: Club Vall Parc (tel: 93 212 67 89; 8am–midnight). Quite expensive.

Water Sports: Base Nautica de la Mar Bella (tel: 93 221 04 32) has all types of boats for hire by qualified sailors; sailing courses and windsurf hire too.

Spectator Sports: Check the daily papers, weekly entertainment guides or magazines such as *El Mundo Deportivo*.

T

TELEPHONES

Phone Numbers: Spain's country code is 34. Barcelona's local area code, 93, must be dialled before all phone numbers, even for local calls.

Public Phones: You can make direct-dial local, national and international calls from public phone booths in the street. Most operate with coins and cards; international phone credit cards can also be used. Instructions for use are given in several languages in the booths.

You can also make calls at public telephone offices called *locutorios*. These are much quieter than making a call on the street and you pay after you have finished the call. The main post office has phone booths.

International Calls: Dial 00 for an international line + the country code + phone number, omitting any initial zero. The country code for the UK is 44, for the US and Canada it is 1, and for Australia, 61. Calls are cheaper after 10pm on weekdays, after 2pm on Saturday, and all day Sunday.

Dial 1009 for operator assistance for calls within Spain, 1008 for assistance within Europe and North Africa and 1005 for the rest of the world.

TIME DIFFERENCES

Spanish time is the same as that in most of Western Europe – Greenwich Mean Time plus one hour. Daylight Savings Time is in effect from the last Sunday in March to the last Sunday in September; clocks go forward one hour in spring and back one hour in autumn, so Spain is generally one hour ahead of London, the same as Paris, and six hours ahead of New York.

TIPPING

There are no golden rules. If you feel the need to leave a tip, make it a token rather than an extravagant one. Some restaurants automatically add a service charge to the total, in which case nothing extra is needed. As a yardstick, in restaurants where a charge is not added, it should be around 5–10 percent and about the same in a taxi. In a bar or café, 80 centimos–€1.50 is enough, depending on the size of the bill.

TOURIST INFORMATION

The main tourist office is Turisme de Barcelona (Plaça de Catalunya 17; tel: 93 285 38 32; from abroad, tel: 93 285 38 34; www.barcelonaturisme.com; Mon–Sat 8am–8pm, Sun 8am–2pm).

The Tourism Information Office in the Ajuntament (Town Hall), Plaça de Sant Jaume, is open Mon–Fri 8.30am–8.30pm, Sat 9am–7pm, Sun and public holidays 9am–2pm.

Informació Turística de Catalunya (Palau Robert, Passeig de Gràcia 107; tel: 93 238 80 91; Mon–Sat 10am–8pm, Sun 10am–2.30pm; www.gencat.cat) gives information about the whole region.

There are also information offices at Sants station (summer daily 8am–8pm, rest of year Mon–Fri 8am–8pm, Sat–Sun 10am–2pm), and the airport (Terminals 1 and 2B; daily 9am–9pm).

There are also several tourist information booths (*cabines*) located at strategic points throughout the city.

Overseas offices:

Canada: 2 Bloor Street West, Suite 3402, Toronto, Ontario, M4W 3E2; tel: 416 961 3131.

UK: 6th floor, 64 North Row, London W1K 7DE; tel: 020 7317 2020. Note that this office is open to the public by appointment only.

US: Water Tower Place, Suite 915 East, 845 North Michigan Avenue, Chicago, IL 60611; tel: 312 642 1992. 8383 Wilshire Boulevard, Suite 960, 90211 Beverly Hills, CA 90211; tel: 323 658 7188.

60 East 42nd Street, 53rd floor, New York, NY 10165; tel: 212 265 8822. 1221 Brickell Avenue, Miami, FL 33131; tel: 305 358 1992.

TOURS

Guides: Licensed English-speaking guides and interpreters may be arranged through the Barcelona Guide Bureau (tel: 93 315 22 61; www.barcelonaguidebureau.com). Hotels and travel agencies also recommend and advise on guides.

Bus Tours: The Barcelona Bus Turístic (www.barcelonabusturistic.cat) offers a tour of 24 city sights with three different routes (Red, Blue and Green), and you can get on and off as you please. Red and Blue depart from Plaça de Catalunya and Green (summer only) from Port Olímpic, between 9 and 9.30am daily. There are full timetables at all stops. The complete journey time is about 2 hours on the Red and Blue route and 40 minutes on the Green. Buy tickets

Toilets
There are many expressions for toilets: *el serveis* or *lavabos* in Catalan; *aseos, servicios* and *WC* ('doobl'-vay') in Castilian. Toilet doors are distinguished by a 'C' for *Caballeros* (gentlemen) or 'S' for *Señoras* (ladies) or by a variety of pictographs. In addition to the well-marked public toilets in main squares and stations, a number of neat coin-operated toilets in portable cabins marked 'WC' are installed around the city. Just about every bar and restaurant has a toilet available for public use. It is considered polite to buy a drink if you drop in to use the conveniences.

on-board or in advance at Turisme de Barcelona (Plaça de Catalunya; tel: 93 285 38 32).

On Foot: Barcelona Walking Tours has English-speaking guided tours of the Barri Gòtic daily at 9.30am. Walks (lasting about 2 hours) begin at Turisme de Barcelona (Plaça de Sant Jaume; tel: 93 285 38 32). At 3pm on Tue, Thur and Sat there is also a Picasso tour that starts from Plaça de Catalunya. Walks should be booked in advance at a tourist office.

By Bicycle: Barcelona by Bicycle (tel: 93 268 21 05) offers tours around El Born, Sant Pere, the Gothic Quarter, the waterfront, and elsewhere.

Out of Town: Popular tours include visits to Montserrat (the mountain monastery some 50km/30 miles from the city), to Sitges, the Penedès wine region and Dalí country – useful if you do not wish to drive in the region.

TRANSPORT

Arrival

By Air: Barcelona's airport is linked by regularly scheduled daily non-stop flights from across Europe. Some flights from the US, Canada and New Zealand are direct; others go through Madrid. Flying time from London is about 2 hours; from New York, it takes about 8 hours.

Iberia, the Spanish national airline, covers most countries in shared arrangements with their national carriers (Iberia House, 10 Hammersmith Broadway, London W6 7AL; tel: 08706 090 500; www.iberia.com). They are a member of Opodo (www.opodo.co.uk), the internet online booking service that gives the cheapest deals among a number of carriers. Good low-cost charter airline deals can be found with easyJet and Ryanair.

The international airport, Barcelona El Prat (tel: 93 298 38 38), is 12km (7 miles) south of the city centre at El Prat de Llobregat and has two terminals, T1 and T2 (A,B,C). There are tourist information and hotel reservation booths in both terminals.

The city can be reached by train or by bus. The national train service, Renfe, runs trains from opposite T2 every half hour, stopping at Estació de Sants, Passeig de Gràcia and Clot, and taking around 20 minutes. The fare is about €3.60. All these stations have metro connections to get you to your final destination. The Aerobús (www.aerobusbcn.com) departs every 10 minutes from both terminals for Plaça de Catalunya (Mon–Sat 6am–1am; €5.30 single, €9.15 return).

Taxis charge about €30 to the city centre. Agree a fare before you start.

By Sea: Barcelona has good sea links to the Balearic Islands and Genoa, Rome and Algiers. Trasmediterránea (Moll Sant Bertran 3; tel: 90 245 46 45; www. trasmediterranea.es) and Balearia (Moll Barcelona; tel: 96 642 87 00; www.balearia.com) operate ferries to the Balearic Islands; the journey takes approximately 8 hours or just 4 hours if you take the express ferry.

By Rail: The Spanish rail network has been greatly modernised. You can take high-speed, sleeper services to Barcelona from several European destinations. The Elipsos Trenhotel arrives at Barcelona's Estació de França from Paris, Milan and Zurich. Progress is ongoing, with a new station due to open in late 2012 at La Sagrera, offering more high-speed links.

Renfe, the Spanish national rail network (tel: 90 232 03 20 for international trains; www.renfe.es), honours Inter-Rail and Eurail cards (the latter sold only outside Europe), and offers substantial discounts for people aged under 26 and over 65.

By Car: The AP7 motorway leads to Barcelona from France 160km (100 miles) to the north. The AP2 leads to Barcelona from Madrid, Zaragoza and Bilbao. From Valencia or the Costa del Sol, take the E-15 north. Your car should display a nationality sticker.

Within Barcelona

Barcelona has a reliable public transport system (see www.tmb.net); getting around town is easy, rapid and inexpensive. Get an up-to-date bus and train *(Feve)* timetable from a tourist information office or metro station. An integrated system means that tickets can be used on buses, trams or trains: best to buy a book of 10 (the *T-10*), which works out about the same as buying six single tickets. The Barcelona Card offers unlimited transport around the city plus free or discounted entry to some museums, shows or tours.

By Bus: Routes and timetables are clearly marked, and maps are available from the tourist office. If it is your first time in the city, you may have trouble recognising where you are, and most bus drivers speak no English. With the metro, it is easier to identify your stop. But buses are a good way of getting to see more of the city. They run daily 5am–11pm (this can vary according to the route); there are infrequent night buses from 10.40pm–5am. For information on buses tel: 93 318 71 74.

By Metro: There are currently 8 metro lines with two further lines under construction, due for completion in 2014. The metro runs Mon–Thur, Sun and public holidays 5am–midnight, Fri 5am–2am, Sat 24 hours. Good pocket-sized maps are available at metro stations. For information on the metro tel: 93 318 70 74.

By Train: Regional FGC (Ferrocarrils Generalitat de Catalunya) trains supplement the metro with urban lines that travel to Barcelona's upper neighbourhoods – Gràcia, Sarrià, Pedralbes and Tibidabo – and to nearby towns such as Terrassa and Sabadell. Unless you are going to one of these destinations, make sure the train you board (most likely at Plaça de Catalunya) is a metro and not an FGC train – it is easy to confuse them. For information on FGC tel: 93 205 15 15; www.fgc.cat.

By Tram: Trams were reinstated in Barcelona in 2004 as an accessible, ecological alternative to the metro.

Above from far left: on board a Golondrina touring boat; cable car from Montjuïc.

There are two lines covering six routes, which mostly service the suburbs. For information on trams tel: 90 219 32 75; www.trambcn.com.

By Taxi: Black and yellow taxis are everywhere and not too expensive. During the day, they are not your best option, as traffic is heavy. At night, especially if you have dined in the Old Town, taxis are the best way to return to your hotel or continue on with the night (have the restaurant call one if you do not feel comfortable waiting on the street). Hail a cab in the street or pick one up where they are lined up (usually outside hotels). A green light and/or a *libre* (vacant) sign shows when the cab is empty.

Reputable taxi companies include Radiotaxi 033 (tel: 93 303 30 33), Taxi Amic (tel: 93 420 80 88) and Barcelona BCN (tel: 93 113 80 88). Check the fare before you get in; rates are fixed and are displayed in several languages on the window. Also ensure that the meter has been reset when you begin your journey. Refuse a cab if the driver claims the meter is not working.

Driving

Car Hire (Rental): Unless you plan to travel a good deal throughout Catalonia, there is no need to hire a car.

Major international companies and Spanish companies have offices in the airport and in the city centre. A value-added tax (IVA) of 18 percent is

Right: the cathedral soars over the Barri Gòtic.

added to the total charge, but will have been included if you have pre-paid before arrival (normally the way to obtain the lowest rates). Fully comprehensive insurance is required and should be included in the price; confirm that this is the case. Most companies require you to pay by credit card, or use your card as a deposit/guarantee. You must be over 21 and have had a licence for at least 6 months. A national driver's licence will suffice for EU nationals; others need an international licence.

Drivers must be able, at any time, to produce a passport, a valid driver's licence, registration papers and Green Card international insurance, which comes with a Bail Bond from your insurance company if you are driving your own car.

Rules and Regulations: Front and rear seat belts are compulsory. Most fines for traffic offences are payable on the spot. Driving rules are the same as those throughout continental Europe: drive on the right, overtake on the left, give right of way to vehicles coming from the right (unless your road is marked as having priority). Do not drink and drive. The permitted blood-alcohol level is low and penalties stiff.

Speed Limits: These are: 120kph (75 mph) on motorways, 100kph (62 mph) on dual carriageways, 90kph (56mph) on main roads, and 50kph (30 mph), or as marked, in urban areas.

Emergencies: In the case of a break-down or other emergency, tel: 112. On motorways there are SOS boxes.

Parking: Finding a place to park can be extremely difficult. Look for 'blue zones' (denoted by a blue 'P'), which are metered areas; or underground parking garages (also marked with a big blue and white 'P'). Green zones are reserved for residents with permits.

V

VISAS AND PASSPORTS

Visas are needed by non-EU nationals unless their country has a reciprocal agreement with Spain. Full information on passport and visa regulations is available from the Spanish Embassy.

W

WEBSITES

- Barcelona Ajuntament (City Hall): www.bcn.es
- Barcelona on the web: www.aboutbarcelona.com
- Barcelona Tourist Information: www.barcelonaturisme.com
- Catalonia on the web: www.gencat.cat
- Spain on the web: www.spaintour.com
- National Tourist Office: www.spain.info
- Transport information: www.tmb.cat

WEIGHTS AND MEASURES

Spain uses the metric system.

Weight/Distance Conversions
To convert kilometres into miles divide by 1.6093; to convert metres into feet divide by 0.3048; to convert kilogrammes into pounds divide by 0.4536; to convert hectares into acres divide by 0.4047. To convert from imperial to metric multiply by the factor shown.
If this all sounds too complicated, it is simpler to bear in mind that a kilometre is roughly five-eighths of a mile; a metre is roughly three feet/one yard; a kilogramme is just over 2lb, a litre is just under two pints, or a fifth of a gallon, and a hectare is about 2½ acres.

Millions of people visit Barcelona each year and there is no shortage of accommodation to suit all tastes and budgets. The 1992 Olympics left a legacy that transformed the hotel scene beyond recognition: old palaces were restored and turned into hotels, sparkling high-rises line the waterfront and run-down establishments have been given a new lease of life. Prices range from very expensive to good-value budget accommodation; and self-catering apartments are becoming very popular.

La Rambla

1898
La Rambla 109; tel: 93 552 95 52; www.hotel1898.com; €€€€
This building was the headquarters of the Philippines Tobacco company until 1898 when the Philippines gained independence from Spain. Now it is a swish hotel with sound-proofed rooms and an up-market colonial elegance.

Citadines Barcelona-Ramblas
La Rambla 122; tel: 93 270 11 11; www.citadines.com; €€€
An excellent-value apartment-hotel with a pleasant breakfast buffet bar and rooftop views. Buy food at the nearby Boquería market *(see p.33)*.

Price guide for a double room for one night with breakfast:	
€€€€	over 200 euros
€€€	140–200 euros
€€	70–140 euros
€	below 70 euros

Continental
La Rambla 138; tel: 93 301 25 70; www.hotelcontinental.com; €€
In a prime position near the top of La Rambla, this is an historic hotel with individual character. Swirling carpets and floral decor can be forgiven when you can sit on a balcony watching the world go by – and at a reasonable price. Ask for a room at the front.

Husa International Cool Local
La Rambla 78–80 ; tel: 93 302 25 66; www.hotelinternationalcool.es; €€–€€€
While retaining its original character outside, the hotel has been completely refurbished within to offer a fresh new minimalist image. Some rooms have a private balcony, and all windows are soundproofed. The rooftop chill-out terrace offers possibly one of the best views over the historic city.

Kabul
Plaça Reial 17; tel: 93 318 51 90; www.kabul.es; €
Long-established youth hostel in a privileged position on this grand square just off La Rambla. Rooms extend to dormitories for up to 20 guests. Known for its party atmosphere.

Oriente
La Rambla 45; tel: 93 302 25 58; www.hotelhusaoriente.com; €€€
Once an old favourite, after refurbishment it has recovered some of its former glory, including the splendid ballroom, but lost some of its personality.

Barri Gòtic

Call

Carrer de l'Arc de Sant Ramon del Call 4; tel: 93 302 11 23; www.hotelcall.es; €

A clean, small, air-conditioned 1-star hotel in the shady lanes of the Barri Gòtic. No bar or restaurant but everything you want is on your doorstep.

Catalonia Portal de l'Angel

Avinguda del Portal de l'Àngel 17; tel: 93 318 41 41; www.hotelescatalonia.es; €€€

Housed in a stylish old building on one of Barcelona's busiest pedestrian shopping streets. Rooms are large and tastefully furnished, and there is a very nice garden patio with a pool.

Gótico

Carrer de Jaume I 14; tel: 93 315 22 11; www.hotelgotico.com; €€€

In one of the Barri Gòtic's main streets, this soundproofed hotel has 81 rooms, some with a terrace, and a sundeck. Thoroughly modern and tasteful, it is handy, light and clean.

Gran Hotel Barcino

Carrer de Jaume I 6; tel: 93 302 20 12; www.hotelbarcino.com; €€

In the heart of the Barri Gòtic, this modern hotel is chic and very well designed. The large, airy lobby does, however, overshadow the rooms.

El Jardí

Plaça de Sant Josep Oriol 1; tel: 93 301 59 00; www.eljardi-barcelona.com; €€

Small hotel overlooking two of the prettiest plazas in Barcelona. The rooms are a bargain, although a plaza view costs a little more. Recently renovated and very popular so book well ahead.

Levante

Baixada de Sant Miquel 2; tel: 93 317 95 65; www.hostallevante.com; €

Basic accommodation with friendly atmosphere. Prides itself on the tale that the young Picasso was a frequent visitor in its former life as a house of ill repute. Just off Carrer d'Avinyó, one of the trendiest streets in the area.

Neri

Carrer de Sant Sever 5; tel: 93 304 06 55; www.hotelneri.com; €€€€

Elegant boutique hotel in a 17th-century palace overlooking one of the most atmospheric squares, near the cathedral. Roof terrace has views over medieval spires. Only 22 rooms.

Nouvel Hotel

Carrer de Santa Ana 18–20; tel: 93 301 82 74; www.hotelnouvel.com; €€€

On a pedestrianised street between La Rambla and Portal d'Àngel, this small hotel has a wonderful Modernista lobby and dining room. Rooms are plainer, but spacious and well equipped.

Ohla

Via Laietana 49; tel: 93 341 50 50; www.ohlahotel.com; €€€€

Opened in 2011, this 5-star hotel occupies a former department store renovated under the guidance of

Above from far left: flowers in reception; Casa Camper *(see p.114)*.

Self-catering
Renting a flat rather than staying in a hotel is becoming ever more popular, especially with families, as they offer the opportunity to self-cater, enabling shopping in the market and cutting holiday costs. Browse websites www.flatsby days.com or www. oh-barcelona.com, which have a range of flats on their books. For a more luxurious option, try www.cru2001.com.

Catalan designer Frederic Amat. Behind its neoclassical facade are monochrome chic interiors, conference facilities, a wellness centre and the Sauc Michelin-starred restaurant. The crowning glory is a rooftop deck with glass-sided pool.

Racó del Pi

Carrer Pi 7; tel: 93 342 6190; www.h10.es; €€€

In the very heart of the Barri Gòtic, around the corner from the Plaça del Pi, this small hotel sits within an old palace. There are only 37 rooms so it tends to get booked up early.

Sant Pere, La Ribera and El Born
Banys Orientals

Carrer de l'Argenteria 37; tel: 93 268 84 60; www.hotelbanysorientals.com; €€

One of the city's best options, with impeccable slick interiors and stylish details, and in the best spot for shopping, wining and dining. On the ground floor is the excellent restaurant Senyor Parellada *(see p.119)*. Unbeatable value, so book well in advance.

Chic&basic

Carrer de la Princesa 50; tel: 93 295 46 52; www.chicandbasic.com; €€–€€€

Rather more chic than basic, this stylish, ultra-modern hotel is situated in a handsome 19th-century building, well located between the Parc de la Ciutadella and the trendy El Born area. Surprisingly good value.

Park Hotel

Avinguda del Marquès de l'Argentera 11; tel: 93 319 60 00; www.park hotelbarcelona.com; €€€

A gem of 1950s architecture, quite rare in Barcelona, opposite the Estació de França, and near the Parc de la Ciutadella. On the edge of the Born district, which is awash with cafés, restaurants and bars and within walking distance of Barceloneta beach.

Pensió 2000

Carrer Sant Pere Més Alt 6, 1st floor; tel: 93 310 7466; www.pensio2000.com; €€

An elegant marble staircase leads to this friendly family-run guesthouse, which is a cut above the average *pension* and right opposite the Palau de la Música Catalana. Great value.

Pension Ciudadela

Carrer del Comercio, 33, 1st floor; tel: 93 319 62 03; www.pension-ciudadela.com; €

Opposite the Estació de França, this humble guesthouse has decent rooms at a very reasonable price, and is within staggering distance of El Born nightlife.

El Raval
Casa Camper

Carrer d'Elisabets 11; tel: 93 342 62 80; www.casacamper.com; €€€

The first hotel to be opened by the sunny Mallorcan shoemakers is as chic as you might expect; 25 rooms designed by Fernando Amat of Vinçon and Jordi Tió in an imposing 19th-century building.

Peak Times
Fortunately for the Northern European and North American tourists who take their holidays in mid-summer, July and August are not considered peak times in hotel terms; September and October are in fact the peak months, when rooms will be more expensive and harder to find.

España

Carrer de Sant Pau 11; tel: 93 550
00 00; www.hotelespanya.com;
€€€

Just off the lower part of La Rambla,
the España retains a flavour of bygone
days. The beautiful public rooms were
designed by the Modernista architect
Domènech i Montaner. The recently
refurbished guest rooms perfectly
blend timeless style with the classicism
of the 19th-century building.

Gat Xino

Carrer Hospital 155, 1st floor; tel: 93
324 88 33; www.gatrooms.es; €€

Almost nursery-school cheerful, this
modern hotel in the city's old hospital
street attracts young clued-up travellers.
The hotel offers single and double
rooms with a 'basic kit' of shower and
toilet. Rooms are not large, but suites
offer extra space. There's a terrace on
the hotel roof for chilling out.

Grau

Carrer Ramelleres 27; tel: 93 301
8135; www.hostalgrau.com; €€

Book early for this popular, well-kept
pension, which is in a good position for
shopping and visiting both the Eixample and Old Town. Excellent
breakfasts in the adjoining bar.

Inglaterra

Carrer de Pelai 14; tel: 93 505 1100;
www.hotel-inglaterra.com; €€€

A contemporary hotel set behind a
handsome old facade, and equally well
located for the bohemian Raval or the
elegant Eixample. Stands out from the
crowd in its price range. The lovely
rooftop terrace offers amazing views.

Peninsular

Carrer de Sant Pau 34; tel: 93 302
31 38; www.hotelpeninsular.net; €

In an old Augustian monastery, with
rooms around a charming inner courtyard. Rooms are basic but good value for
money, and staff are helpful and friendly.

The Waterfront

Arts

Passeig de la Marina 19–21; tel: 93
221 10 00: www.hotelartsbarcelona.
com; €€€€

A high-tech, ultra-deluxe high-rise,
situated right by the beach in Vila
Olímpica. Extremely efficient, decorated with sophisticated, understated
taste. Large rooms, huge bathrooms
and amazing views.

Barcelona Princess

Avinguda Diagonal 1; tel: 93 356
10 00; www.princess-hotels.com;
€€€€

On the cutting edge in all senses:
designed by leading Catalan architect
Oscar Tusquets, situated in the rejuvenated district of the Diagonal Mar,
and offering all possible facilities.
Prices are subject to radical cuts, so it

Price guide for a double room
for one night with breakfast:

€€€€	over 200 euros
€€€	140–200 euros
€€	70–140 euros
€	below 70 euros

Sea Views

There are several additional hotels along the rejuvenated waterfront near Diagonal Mar where high standard accommodation can be found at a reasonable price. As they are a taxi or metro ride from the centre, they are less popular, but the advantage of sea views and more peaceful nights is well worth considering.

is worth trying to bargain for the benefit of sleeping at this giddy height, with great views of sea and city.

Duquesa de Cardona

Passeig de Colom 12; tel: 93 268 90 90; www.hduqesadecardona.com; €€€

A classically elegant hotel set in the long-overlooked, handsome buildings giving on to the original waterfront and the old harbour. The pool and terrace on the roof are a hidden treasure. Luxury at a moderate price.

Equity Point Sea

Plaça del Mar 4; tel: 93 231 20 45; www.equity-point.com; €

An unbeatable position for a youth hostel, right on Barceloneta beach. This chain of youth hostels also has a branch in La Ribera (Point Gothic) and one up in Gràcia (Point Centric).

Front Marítim

Passeig de García Faria 69–71; tel: 93 303 44 40; www.hotelfront maritim.com; €€–€€€

On the waterfront between the Vila Olímpica and Diagonal Mar. It is just a taxi ride away from the inner city buzz, but you wake up to sea views. Slick and comfortable.

The Eixample

Actual

Carrer del Rosselló 238; tel: 93 552 05 50; www.hotelactual.com; €€€

Situated on the same block as Gaudí's La Pedrera, this well-equipped, contemporary hotel offers minimalist decor

in dark brown and white combined with a warm, personal atmosphere. It is sought after, so book well in advance.

Balmes Hotel

Carrer de Mallorca 216; tel: 93 451 19 14; www.derbyhotels.com; €€€

The Balmes promises 'the advantages of the countryside in the heart of the city', and has an attractive leafy garden and a pool. Good location.

Casa Fuster

Passeig de Gràcia 132; tel: 93 255 30 00; www.hotelescenter.es; €€€€

Classified as a five-star 'Monument' hotel, Casa Fuster, built by Domènech i Montaner in 1908, has been restored to its Modernista splendour. Facilities include the Café Viennese, the Galaxó restaurant, a jacuzzi and gym, plus a roof terrace pool, from where there are gorgeous views. A member of the Leading Small Hotels of the World.

Circa 1905

Carrer de Provenza 286; tel: 93 505 69 60; www.circa1905.com; €€€

This well-kept secret on the first floor of a Modernista building offers a privileged location from which to explore Catalan Modernism. Just nine renovated rooms, some of which have balconies.

Condes de Barcelona

Passeig de Gràcia 75; tel: 93 445 00 00; www.condesdebarcelona. com; €€€–€€€€

Contemporary elegance in two Modernista buildings facing each other in

the Quadrat d'Or area of the Eixample. The two Michelin-starred Lasarte restaurant is under the watchful eye of celebrated Basque chef Martìn Berasategui. There is a roof terrace with a mini pool.

Constanza

Carrer del Bruc 33; tel: 93 270 19 10; www.hotelconstanza.com; €€

Modern, efficient boutique hotel that should appeal to those with a funky youthful outlook. The rooms are not huge, but some have terraces.

Girona

Carrer de Girona 24, 1st floor; tel: 93 265 02 59; www.hostalgirona.com; €

A grand stone staircase rises from the elegant patio of this Modernista building designed by Idelfons Cerdà and situated in the area known as the Quadrat d'Or. The hostal is a good-value option in a very central location, with a warm, friendly reception from the Berlanga family.

Gran Hotel Havana Silken

Gran Vía de les Corts Catalanes 647; tel: 93 341 70 00; www.hotelessilken.com; €€€

Classic and sophisticated style runs through this 1872 mansion. Barcelona's signature design elements are displayed in all the bedrooms, and on the panoramic roof terrace with a pool.

Granvía

Gran Vía de les Corts Catalanes 642; tel: 93 318 19 00; www.nnhotels.com; €€€

Housed in a neoclassical building that was constructed as a bourgeois palace, today the Granvia's rooms feature original 19th-century furnishings that ooze elegance and distinction. Very close to the Plaça de Catalunya and Passeig de Gràcia.

Omm

Carrer del Rosselló 265; tel: 93 445 40 00; www.hotelomm.es; €€€€

Just off Passeig de Gràcia, this award-winning designer hotel is part of the seriously cool Tragaluz group. The rooms are stylish and well lit, and the rooftop pool is stunning, with views of Gaudí's La Pedrera. The in-house club is reckoned one of the best places to be on Barcelona's night scene.

Paseo de Gracia

Passeig de Gràcia 102; tel: 93 215 06 03; www.hotelpaseodegracia.es; €€

Another vestige from the past, with some original fittings. In the same block as La Pedrera, it is in a prime location and good value for money in this expensive area.

The 5 Rooms

Carrer de Pau Claris 72, 1st floor; tel: 93 342 78 80; www.thefiverooms. com; €€

As the name suggests, just five guest rooms make up this romantic bed-and-breakfast place, tucked away in the heart of the Eixample neighbourhood. Stylish, modern and thoughtfully decorated, it bills itself as a 'cocooning' concept to make you feel at home.

RESTAURANTS

Barcelona offers the world on a plate, with cuisines from around the globe. It is, however, Catalan food that catches the imagination, with an emphasis on first-class seasonal and fresh produce, used from Michelin-starred establishments to humble tapas bars. Choose from the elegant surroundings of five-star hotels, seafood restaurants with a beach view, sleek modern bistros and tiny tapas bars, or explore the backstreets for traditional family-run restaurants, where time has stood still.

La Rambla

Amaya
La Rambla 20–4; tel: 93 302 10 37; www.restauranteamaya.com; daily 1–4pm, 7–11.30pm; €€€

A Basque restaurant run by the fourth generation of the Torralba family. The cosy dining room stays true to its original style and there is a lovely terrace.

Egipte
La Rambla 79; tel: 93 317 95 45; www.egipte-ramblas.com; daily noon–1am; €

A lively, popular place just near the Boqueria. Once a small eatery within the market itself, Egipte is now spread over several floridly decorated floors.

Price guide for a three-course à la carte dinner for one with a bottle of house wine:

€€€€	over 60 euros
€€€	40–60 euros
€€	25–40 euros
€	below 25 euros

Fresc Co
Carrer del Carme 16; tel: 93 301 68 37; daily 12.45pm–1am; €

Just past the church of Betlem, this is one in a chain of self-service restaurants offering all you can eat for under €10.

Barri Gòtic

Agut
Carrer d'en Gignàs 16; tel: 93 315 17 09; Tue–Sat 1–4pm, 8.30–11.30pm, Sun 1.30–4pm; €€

This historic restaurant is hidden down a small street. Relaxed, with a bohemian feel, it has plenty of Catalan flavour and lots of specials. The excellent huge rice dishes are meant to be shared.

Can Culleretes
Carrer d'en Quintana 5; tel: 93 317 30 22; www.culleretes.com; Tue–Sat 1.30–4pm, 9–11pm, Sun 1.30–4pm, closed mid-July to mid-Aug; €–€€

Barcelona's oldest restaurant has served traditional Catalan food since 1786. It is cosy and informal, and has tasty classics including *espinacas à la catalana* (spinach with pine nuts and raisins).

Los Caracoles
Carrer d'Escudellers 14; tel: 93 301 20 41; www.loscaracoles.es; daily 1.15pm–midnight; €€–€€€€

'The Snails' is famous for the chicken on spits outside. It has been around since 1835. Touristy but fun, and you can get fish, game, chicken or lamb, in addition to the speciality *caracoles*.

Limbo
Carrer de la Mercè 13; tel: 93 310 76

99; www.limborestaurante.com; Mon 1.30–4pm, Tue–Fri 1.30–4pm, 8.30–11.30pm, Sat 8.30–11.30pm; €€–€€€

An imaginative menu of Mediterranean dishes draws customers back again and again to this intimate space.

Shunka

Carrer del Sagristans 5; tel: 93 412 49 91; daily 1.30–3.30pm, 8.30–11.30pm; €€€

Hidden behind the cathedral is one of the best Japanese restaurants in the city. Love and wisdom goes into the preparation of top-quality specialities right in front of your eyes.

Sant Pere, La Ribera, El Born and Ciutadella

Cal Pep

Plaça de les Olles 8; tel: 93 310 79 61; www.calpep.com; Tue–Fri 1–3.45pm, 7.30–11.30pm, Mon 7.30–11.30pm, Sat 1–3.45pm; €€€

A boisterous bar in El Born that does some of the best seafood in Barcelona. Join the cava-sipping queue for a seat at the counter where you can watch delectable little dishes being prepared.

Espai Sucre

Carrer de la Princesa 53; tel: 93 268 16 30; www.espaisucre.com; Tue–Sat 9–11.30pm; €€€

Desserts only are served at this inventive restaurant. However, they include 'salads', 'soups' and other concoctions never found in a cake shop – or anywhere else. Excellent dessert wines accompany the 3- to 5-course meals.

Passadis de Pep

Plaça de Palau 2; tel: 93 310 10 21; www.passadis.com; Mon–Sat 1.30–3.30pm, 9–11.30pm; €€€€

A rustic restaurant with no menu – they just keep bringing you the dishes – which presents skilfully cooked seafood using the freshest ingredients; a culinary experience for fish lovers.

Senyor Parellada

Carrer de l'Argentería 37; tel: 93 310 50 94; www.senyorparellada.com; daily 1–4pm, 8.30pm–midnight; €€–€€€

An attractive, popular spot owned and run by the family that owns the adjoining Banys Orientals hotel. The purely Catalan menu is based on unpretentious home-made dishes.

7 Portes

Passeig d'Isabel II; tel: 93 319 30 33; www.7portes.com; daily 1pm–1am; €€

Sympathetically restored, recapturing the original atmosphere, this 160-year-old classic specialises in rice dishes, one for each day of the week.

El Raval

L'Antic Forn

Carrer del Pintor Fortuny 28; tel: 93 412 02 86; www.lanticforn.com; Mon–Sat 9am–5pm, 8pm–midnight; €–€€

The 'Old Bakery' is an informal place spread over different spaces, which enjoys a good reputation for Catalan cuisine that won't disappoint you, at affordable prices.

Above from far left: La Tinaja bodega in El Born (Carrer de l'Espartería 9); chocolate bars by Brunells; tapas menu; smart dining at seafood restaurant Carballeira (Carrer de la Reina Cristina 3).

Menú del Día Lunch can be the most economical meal of the day, with nearly every restaurant offering a set menu comprising a starter, main course of meat or fish, a dessert and a glass of wine, a beer or a soft drink. Prices and quality vary, of course, but you should be able to eat well and substantially for around €10–15.

Time to Eat

To get the most out of the cuisine in Barcelona, try to eat at the same time as local people. Thus, breakfast only tends to be hearty when eaten mid-morning; earlier starts are more likely to feature coffee and biscuits. Lunch is the main meal of the day and eaten at about 2–3pm; dinner is a slightly lighter affair, served from around 9–10pm. If this seems like too long a wait, try having tapas with a drink, or visiting one of the many pastry shops around the city for an indulgently creamy cake.

Casa Leopoldo

Carrer de Sant Rafael 24; tel: 93 441 30 14; www.casaleopoldo.com; Tue–Sat 1.30–3.30pm, 8.30–10.30pm, Sun 1.30–3.30pm; €€€

Tucked away in the Barri Xino, this place serves excellent Catalan stews.

Elisabets

Carrer d'Elisabets 2; tel: 93 317 58 26; Mon–Fri 8am–11pm; €

Bustling local bar popular for generous home-made dishes and a good-value set menu.

La Reina del Raval

Rambla del Raval 5; tel: 93 443 36 55; daily 1.30–3.30pm, 8.30–11pm; €€–€€€

With big windows looking onto the Rambla, this bright modern space has a young clientele and features an eclectic menu with market ingredients. There is a gourmet menu, an à la carte and a lunch-time set menu, plus tapas.

Sesamo

Carrer de Sant Antoni Abat 52; tel: 93 441 64 11; Tue–Sun 8am–midnight; €

Close to Sant Antoni market, this inviting vegetarian place sells good spicy dishes. The tasting menu is a delight.

The Waterfront

Agua

Passeig Marítim 30; tel: 93 225 12 72; www.aguadeltragaluz.com; daily 1–4pm, 8–11.30pm; €€–€€€

Almost on the beach, with tables indoors and out, the modern, attractive Agua gets very busy, especially at lunch time, so booking is essential. Well-prepared fish and seafood, rice dishes, and imaginative vegetarian dishes.

Barceloneta

Carrer de l'Escar 22; tel 93 221 21 11; www.rte.barceloneta.co.uk; daily 1–4pm, 8.30pm–1am; €€€

The outdoor terrace, jutting out above the fishing boats and smooth yachts of Port Vell, makes this one of the most perfect places to eat seafood dishes.

La Oca Mar

Espigó Bac de Roda, Platja Mar Bella; tel: 93 225 01 00; daily 1pm–1am; €€

This spectacular restaurant, situated right on the breakwater, virtually in the sea, serves a range of well-prepared seafood and seasonal local dishes.

Travi del Port

Moll de Gregal, Local 33, 1st floor; tel: 93 225 99 66; www.gruptravi.com; daily 1pm–1am; €€–€€€

In the Olympic Port, this dependable restaurant serves well-prepared, if fairly predictable, Mediterranean dishes. Views of the port are superb.

Xiringuíto Escribà

Avinguda del Litoral Mar 42, Platja del Bogatell; tel: 93 221 07 29; www.escriba.es; daily noon–5pm; €€€

Lots of imaginative fish and rice dishes in this family-run establishment by the beach. The Escribà family is renowned for chocolates and pastries, so the puddings are guaranteed to be marvellous.

The Eixample

Alkimia

Carrer de la Indústria 79; tel: 93 207 61 15; www.alkimia.cat; Mon–Fri 1.30–3.30pm, 8.30–11pm; €€€€

Near the Sagrada Família, this is a shining example of the new talent in Catalan cuisine. Renowned Michelin-starred chef Jordi Vilà is the alchemist, working wonders on ordinary Catalan dishes. Fast becoming one of Barcelona's leading restaurants.

Casa Calvet

Carrer de Casp 48; tel: 93 412 40 12; www.casacalvet.es; Mon–Sat 1–3.30pm, 8.30–11pm; €€€–€€€€

On the first floor of one of Gaudí's first apartment buildings, Casa Calvet exudes elegant Modernista ambience. Tables are spaced well apart; some even occupy private booths, and the excellent Catalan menu is fairly priced.

El Caballito Blanco

Carrer de Mallorca 196; tel: 93 453 96 16; Tue–Sat 1.15–3.45pm, 8.45–10.45pm, Sun 1.15–3.45pm; €€€€

An old-fashioned, popular place, using fresh seasonal ingredients. It is a relief to find places like this have escaped being redesigned and relaunched.

Gorría

Carrer de la Diputació 421; tel: 93 245 11 64; www.restaurantegorria. com; Mon–Sat 1–3.30pm, 9–11.30pm (closed Mon pm); €€€

Daily deliveries of fish from the north make this family-run place the perfect spot to eat quality Basque dishes.

Jaume de Provença

Carrer de Provença 88; tel: 93 430 00 29; www.jaumeprovenza.com; Tue–Sat 1–3.45pm, 9–11.15pm, Sun 1–3.45pm; €€€–€€€€

A small restaurant with a country flavour, near Sants station, named after innovative owner-chef Jaume Bargués. After nearly 30 years it is still considered to be a pioneer of creative cuisine and is correspondingly popular.

L'Olive

Carrer de Balmes 47; tel: 93 452 19 90; www.rte-olive.com; Mon–Sat 1–4pm, 8.30–midnight, Sun 1–4pm; €€€

L'Olive has long been considered a fashionable place for classic Catalan dishes with an original touch, served in slick minimalist premises.

Moments

Hotel Mandarin Oriental, Passeig de Gràcia 38–48; tel: 93 151 87 81; www.mandarinoriental.com; Tue–Sat 1.30–3.30pm, 8.30–10.30pm; €€€€

Overseen by Carme Ruscalleda, the only female chef in the world to hold six Michelin stars, Moments stands out for its refreshing twist on Catalan dishes served amid stunning decor.

Tragaluz

Passatge de la Concepció 5; tel: 93 487 06 21; www.grupotragaluz.com; daily 1.30–4pm, 8.30pm–midnight; €€€–€€€€

An extensive, creative menu of Mediterranean food in a trendy restaurant where you can dine under a glass roof.

Above from far left: the new and old faces of dining in Barcelona, at Bilbao Berria (Carrer Argentería 6) and Els Quatre Gats (see p.37).

Seafood
Peix (fish) and *marisc* (shellfish) should not be missed; a *graellada* (mixed grill) allows you to sample several dishes at once and is a good option for two to share. For paella, it is worth going to a good restaurant, as cheap imitations are usually disappointing and not representative of the great seafood on offer here.

To find out what's on pick up the free magazines *Barcelona Connect* (www.barcleonaconnect.com) and *Metropolitan* (www.barcelona-metropolitan.com), which are published monthly in English and are available in bars, restaurants, hotels and many other venues.

Theatres

L'Antic Teatre
Carrer de Verdaguer i Callís 12; tel: 93 315 23 54; www.anticteatre.com
Hidden away with a pleasant bar terrace, L'Antic hosts touring companies and local performers. Expect anything from mime to circus, plus plays and films.

Sala Beckett
Carrer de Ca l'Alegre de Dalt 55; tel: 93 284 53 12; www.salabeckett.com
Inspired by Samuel Beckett, this small theatre is big on challenging performances, promoting Catalan playwrights and works from around the world.

Teatre Lliure
Plaça Margarida Xirgú 1; tel: 93 289 27 70; www.teatrelliure.com
With its own resident company under the direction of the dynamic Àlex Rigola, this theatre has an adventurous programme of theatre and dance.

Teatre Nacional de Catalunya
Plaça de les Arts 1; tel: 93 306 57 00; www.tnc.cat
Supported by the government, all plays here promote the Catalan language. The remit, however, is also to stage dance, opera, music, circus and puppetry.

Music

L'Auditori
Carrer de Lepant 150; tel: 93 247 93 00; www.auditori.com
Hosting such top-class names as Lang Lang, and with its own prestigious orchestra, this purpose-built venue has a good reputation for classical music.

Gran Teatre del Liceu
La Rambla 51–9; tel: 93 485 99 13; www.liceubarcelona.cat
Barcelona's opera house is considered one of the world's finest. Top names in opera, plus jazz, big bands and more.

Harlem Jazz Club
Carrer de Comtessa de Sobradiel 8, tel: 93 310 07 55; www.harlemjazzclub.es
In the heart of the old town, this intimate space is perfect for nights of jazz, soul and funk. Later in the evening the DJs start spinning their decks.

Jamboree
Plaça Reial 17; tel: 93 319 17 89; www.masimas.com/jamboree
Renowned club headlining some of the best names in jazz, open every night with jam sessions on Mondays; also nights with Latin and tropical vibes.

Palau de la Música Catalana
Carrer de St Francesc de Paula 2; tel: 902 442 882; www.palaumusica.org
This wonderful Modernista building houses a beautiful main hall for concerts and recitals. The modern extension has perfect acoustics for chamber music.

Razzmatazz

Carrer de Pamplona 88/Carrer dels Almogàvers 122; tel: 93 320 82 00; www.salarazzmatazz.com

A primary venue for live music, these two locations in Poble Nou comprise five different clubs. All genres of popular music can be enjoyed here.

Los Tarantos

Plaça Reial 17; tel: 93 319 17 89; www.masimas.com/tarantos

Located above Jamboree, this is the oldest flamenco club in Barcelona. You can watch a 30-minute taster show, but check for times beforehand.

Mercat de les Flors

Carrer de Lleida 59; tel: 93 426 18 75; www.mercatflors.cat

Promoting a range of contemporary dance and emerging new talent, this lively venue is located in the old summer flower market building.

Cinema Maldà

Carrer del Pi 5; tel: 93 481 37 04; www.cinemamalda.net

A popular central venue for arthouse and original language version (VO) films with Spanish/Catalan subtitles.

Filmoteca de Catalunya

Plaça Salvador Seguí 1–9; tel: 93 567 10 70; www.filmoteca.cat

In the bohemian El Raval district, this government-funded cinema screens films from around the world. Has a film archive, exhibitions and a café.

Bars and Clubs

Bar Marsella

Carrer de Sant Pau 65; tel: 93 442 72 63; no website

Open since 1820 and the haunt of the likes of Picasso and Gaudí, this atmospheric bar is legendary for its absinthe – and tourists still flock to try it.

Hotel Duquesa de Cardona

Passeig de Colom 12; tel: 93 268 90 90; www.hduquesadecardona.com

The roof terrace has one of the best views in the city. In summer it's a great, if somewhat pricey, place for a cocktail.

Marmalade

Carrer de la Riera Alta 4–6: tel: 93 442 39 66; www.marmaladebarcelona.com

Check out this local hotspot in trendy El Ravel. It's beautifully decked out, echoing a 1950s feel, with plush sofas and chrome-backed bar.

Sotavento

Passeig Maritim de la Barceloneta 38: tel 902 226 788; www.sotaventobcn.com

One of several lively beach clubs along this stretch (check out Opium Mar at No. 34), which features a lounge dance club on the seafront terrace.

Sutton Club

Carrer de Tuset 13; tel: 93 414 42 17; www.suttonmusicclub.com

Ultra-cool, up-market club where you can dress up to the nines, Sutton features three large bars and a separate dance floor.

Above from far left: Teatre Nacional de Catalunya; Bar Marsella; Harlem Jazz Club; Palau de la Música Catalana.

CREDITS

Insight Step by Step Barcelona
Written by: Roger Williams
Updated by: Jackie Staddon and Hilary Weston
Commissioning Editor: Catherine Dreghorn
Copy-editor: Pam Barrett
Series Editor: Carine Tracanelli
Cartography: Apa Cartography Department
Picture Researcher: Richard Cooke
Production: Tynan Dean, Linton Donaldson and Rebeka Ellam

Photography by: Apa: Annabel Elston, Jon Santa Cruz, Jeroen Sniders, Bill Wassman and Gregory Wrona except: Alamy 23tl, 44, 69tr; Corbis 2/3, 7tr, 7br, 11br, 12tr, 22tl, 22tr, 23tr, 30bl, 34tr, 38b, 68tr, 72tl, 73tl, 80bl, 82tl, 84tl, 90t, 92t, 93t, 93br, 102–3; Fotolia 4/5, 21tl, Mike Merchant 63tl; MNAC 24t, 78tr; Ingrid Morató 46l (c, t, b); Photoasia 25t, 25b; Prisma Archivo Fotográfico 24bl; Turisme de Barcelona/G. Foto 110b; Turisme de Barcelona/J. Trullàs 110t.
Cover: main image: age fotostock/SuperStock; front left: Stuart Pitkin/istock photo; front right: Gregory Wrona/Apa.

Printed by: CTPS – China

© 2012 Apa Publications (UK) Ltd.

Second Edition 2012

www.insightguides.com

DISTRIBUTION

Worldwide
**APA Publications GmbH & Co Verlag KG
(Singapore branch)**
7030 Ang Mo Kio Ave 5
08-65 Northstar @ AMK
Singapore 569880
apasin@singnet.com.sg

UK and Ireland
**Dorling Kindersley Ltd,
a Penguin Group company**
80 Strand, London WC2R 0RL, UK
customerservice@dk.com

United States
Ingram Publisher Services
One Ingram Blvd
PO Box 3006
La Vergne, TN 37086-1986
customer.service@ingrampublisherservices.com

Australia
Universal Publishers
PO Box 307
St Leonards NSW 1590
sales@universalpublishers.com.au

New Zealand
Brown Knows Publications
11 Artesia Close, Shamrock Park
Auckland, New Zealand 2016
sales@brownknows.co.nz

CONTACTING THE EDITORS

We would appreciate it if readers would alert us
to errors or outdated information by writing to
us at insight@apaguide.co.uk or Apa Publications,
PO Box 7910, London SE1 1WE, UK.

INDEX

TMB

S5 Sant Cugat-R
S55 Universitat A
S2 Sabadell
S1 Terrassa

Les Planes

Baixador de Vallvidrera
Vallvidrera Superior
Carretera de les Aigües
Peu del Funicular
Vallvidrera Inferior

Túnel de Vallvidrera
Ronda de Dalt
CosmoCaixa

R Molins de Rei
R1 Molins de Rei
R4 Sant Vicenç de Calders

T3 Sant Feliu | Consell Comarcal
Torreblanca
Walden
Rambla de Sant Just
Hospital Sant Joan Despí | TV3
A-2 (Lleida-Tarragona)

Reina Elisenda
L6
L3 Zona Universitària
Av Esplugues
Pg Reina Elisenda

Av. Tibidabo
L7
Sarrià
Pl John F. Kennedy

T2 Llevant | Les Planes
La Fontsanta
Centre Miquel Martí i Pol
Pont d'Esplugues

Les Tres Torres
La Bonano
Muntar
Vila
Aigü
St. Gerva

T1 Bon Viatge
Fontsanta Fatjó
La Sardana
Montesa
El Pedró
Ignasi Iglésias

Can Clota
Ca n'Oliveres
Zona Universitària
Palau Reial

Pius XII
Maria Cristina
Numància
L'Illa

S4 Martorell-Enllaç
S8 Olesa de Montserrat
R5 Manresa-Baixador
R6 Igualada
S3 Can Ros

Les Aigües
Cornellà
L5
Cornellà Centre

Sant Ildefons
Can Boixeres
Can Vidalet
Can Serra
Pubilla Cases
Florida

Can Rigal
Av. de Xile

Palau Reial
Maria Cristina
Les Corts
Plaça del Centre

Francesc Macià
T1 T2 T3
Gràcia

L8 Molí Nou-Ciutat Cooperativa
Sant Boi
Cornellà-Riera
Gavarra
Almeda

Ctra de l'Hospitalet
l'Hospitalet de Llobregat

Ernest Lluch
Collblanc

Entença
Hospital Clínic
Provença

R3 l'Hospitalet-Av. Carrilet
R Rbla. Just Oliveras
Av. Carrilet

Torrassa
Santa Eulàlia
Mercat Nou

Badal
Plaça de Sants
Barcelona-Sants
Sants Estació

Tarragona
Pl Leta

R R2 Castelldefels
R2 Sant Vicenç de Calders
Sud

L1
Hospital de Bellvitge

St Josep
Bellvitge
Gornal
Europa Fira

Hostafrancs
Espanya
Rocafort Urgell Universita

Sant Antoni
Plaça Catalunya
Catalunya

Gavà Viladecans
El Prat de Llobregat

Ildefons Cerdà
Magòria La Campana

L8 Espanya
S33 S4 S8
R5 R6

Poble Sec

L6 Cat
L7 Cat

R R2 Aeroport
Nord

Parc de Montjuïc
L2 Paral·lel
S1 S
S5 S
Paral·lel

Castell de Montjuïc
Mirador
Paral·lel
Miramar
Dras

Jaume I
St. Sebast

© Ferrocarril Metropolità de Barcelona, S.A. Tots els drets reservats.

Codi Código Key

	Estació de ferrocarril / Estación de ferrocarril / Railway station		Telefèric / Teleférico / Cable-car
	Tren d'Alta Velocitat / Tren de Alta Velocidad / High Speed Train		Centres TMB d'atenció al ciutadà / Centros TMB de atención al ciudadano / TMB Citizen service centers
	Estació d'autobusos / Estación de autobuses / Bus station		Estació / Estación / Station
	Estació Marítima / Estación Marítima / Seaboard station		Estació terminal / Estación terminal / Terminus station
	Tramvia Blau / Tranvía azul / Blue Tram		Estació de correspondència / Estación de correspondencia / Connecting station
	Funicular / Funicular / Funicular railway		Correspondència L9/L10 / Correspondencia L9/L10 / L9/L10 connecting

Tota la Xarxa de Metro de TMB és accessible, excepte les estacions següents:

Toda la Red de Metro de TMB es accesible, excepto las siguientes estaciones:

The entire TMB underground network is adapted, except the following stations:

L1
Rbla. Just Oliveras
Plaça de Sants
Espanya
Urquinaona
Clot

L3
Zona Universitària
Espanya
Poble Sec
Passeig de Gràcia
Vallcarca

L4
Maragall
Verdaguer
Urquinaona
Jaume I
Ciutadella | Vila Ol
Bogatell
Llacuna
Poblenou

L5
Virrei Amat
Maragall
Verdaguer
Plaça de Sants
Collblanc